CONDUCTING TECHNIQUE

CONDUCTING TECHNIQUE

For Beginners and Professionals

BROCK McELHERAN

NEW YORK

OXFORD UNIVERSITY PRESS

1966

Copyright © 1964, 1966 by Brock McElheran
Library of Congress Catalogue Card Number: 66-21847
10
Printed in the United States of America

FOREWORD

Should we teach conducting? Are there not far too many conductors in the world of music today? The student bent on conducting is often the least worthy and the least promising. He is the kind who, instead of working on himself and improving his musicianship, dreams of working on others, dreams of baton glory, podium glory, of elegantly illustrating the music with the drama of his gestures. In short, should we encourage the conducting mania? In answer to these misgivings there is this to say: True, there are legions of conductors and conductorial aspirants, but there is a distinct shortage of good conductors. The writer of this book is one. He has impressed me more than once by the lucid and inventive approach to conducting problems, by the ease with which he teaches performers some very complex and novel performing tasks. He has never succumbed to the vainglorious attitude mentioned above which has made the conducting profession intellectually suspect. He is dedicated and devoted to the music he is performing and the performing group he is conducting.

This double dedication lies at the root of the profession. Mr. McElheran's book starts at the very beginning and ends with some remarkably profound insights on conductorial subtleties. He includes all music; even our so-called *avant-garde* is within his scope. He realizes that we are heading toward a new type of conductor, one who performs a difficult task indeed: the unraveling of new music, of new notations, the teaching of new methods to helpless, though often professional, performers. It is my feeling that a conductor is primarily a teacher; at least, teaching is his primary function at rehearsals. He holds the score in his hands. The individual performer has but his own part. Interpretation, yes, but essentially conducting is teaching, making the notes work. Essential here is the conductor's inner vision: what the sound at a given moment should be. At this point the ears take over—detect the error, make a quick diagnosis, find and propose a remedy. An experienced conductor is one in whom this threefold action—detection, diagnosis, remedy—takes place simultaneously, almost in a flash: as he hears the error, he realizes where the fault lies and what to do about it. This book gives valuable hints about these three basic conductorial functions, and it gives these from the viewpoint of chorus and orchestra alike. The uniqueness of this book can be traced back to the current instrumental point of departure. A well-rounded conductor is at home in all music, choral and orchestral, old and new. Mr. McElheran's personal musicianship sets an example here; so does the firmness combined with gentle humor with which he leads the student toward mastery of the problems at hand. Conductors, wise ones, use just these methods to obtain the best from their musicians. Let no one forget that a conductor, just like a teacher, is only as good as the result he obtains from the work of others.

LUKAS FOSS

PREFACE

Most books on conducting either slight conducting technique itself or else delve deeply into every possible complexity which the human brain can conceive. It is hoped that this small volume will help train young conductors or improve experienced professionals by concentrating primarily on conducting technique without being unduly abstruse.

Several concepts are stated which have not appeared in print before, as far as is known. While following internationally accepted general principles of conducting, certain modifications in beat patterns and other technical matters are described which are felt to be more scientific than those frequently encountered. These have proven invaluable in performance. A few cows held sacred in some quarters are examined and dealt with in what is hoped is a reasonably humane manner.

The book is designed to be used by both choral and instrumental conductors, and by beginners and professionals (that is, anyone who is regularly employed in the conducting field, including school, university, church, concert, and opera musicians.) It is felt that the beginner, with some help from a friend or preferably a teacher, can start his training with this as a textbook, while the advanced musician will find much to cause him to re-examine his thinking and possibly revise his conducting habits. At the end of each chapter are separate assignments for beginners and for professionals desiring to strengthen any weaknesses.

With beginners, the suggested course of instruction should last several months; they must not be rushed. It takes time to form a secure, facile and almost instinctive technique. The professional may read the entire book in an evening, picking up a few suggestions here and there, or devote several weeks to practising.

Certain 20th century techniques are introduced at an early stage. It is found that this develops a more solid foundation for contemporary music than when left until later, as is the case in most older texts (if not ignored completely).

The musical illustrations are extremely simple, being mostly pitchless rhythms. It is felt that the complicated motions of conducting are more easily understood if at first applied to such fragments, rather than to the highly complex examples sometimes used. Similar passages are given as technical exercises. More can be written by the student or teacher in a few minutes. While not artistic, they bear the same relation to conducting that études or *vocalises* do to solo performance.

In no cases is it necessary to turn to musical examples outside this volume in order to understand the text. Authors who constantly urge readers to "look up the third movement of so-and-so's such-and-such" show a lack of understanding of the undergraduate mind and also of library hours.

Many of the technical drills suggested can profitably be practised alone, or with only one or two friends as guinea pigs. One reason is to help a beginner gain security before being subjected to the terrifying gaze of a group and the devastating comments of his professor. Moreover, too many conducting teachers expect their students to develop technique in the few minutes per month in which they can conduct a large organization. One of the most important principles of the writer's method is to practise conducting much as one would an instrument. Many suggestions are given along this line.

Describing motions in words is difficult. Hence it is hoped that the reader will use a large amount of common sense in applying the principles herein stated, especially in unusual situations. The latter have usually been omitted, partly to save space and partly because the directions for conducting a highly complicated passage are usually harder to figure out than the problem itself. Attempting to cross all the possible bridges in the world in advance is a tedious waste of time.

In arranging the order of chapters an attempt has been made to insulate those on highly technical subjects by interspersing others of a more general nature. This provides more time for the assimilation of the intricate physical actions, as well as variety of reading. An instructor may assign the chapters in a different order without difficulty.

The first poor cow to be destroyed is the Italian plural of such common words as "concerto." This book will use "s," as in "pianos." Countless musicians say "concerti" and "celli" but never "viole" and "sonate"!

May I express my deepest indebtedness to the four conducting teachers with whom I studied formally—Ettore Mazzoleni, Nicholas Goldschmidt, Stanley Chapple, and the late Pierre Monteux; the many conducting greats and not-so-greats from whom I have learned so many do's and don't's; the seven hundred students, young and less young, who have patiently listened to these words over the years and can now read them; the numerous orchestras and choirs who have proved to me what works and what doesn't; and finally my wife, for things too numerous to mention, including many of the important points under the chapter on nerves!

BROCK MCELHERAN

Potsdam, N.Y.
February 1966

CONTENTS

CONDUCTING TECHNIQUE

CHAPTER I

INSPIRATION

The most important requirement in a conductor is the ability to inspire the performers. This might be given other names: leadership, hypnotic power, contagious enthusiasm, or just good teaching ability (for a rehearsal is simply a class in which the conductor teaches the performers how to play the music). Perhaps it is best described in a simple phrase: MAKING THE PERFORMERS WANT TO DO THEIR BEST.

The point seems so obvious as to be almost trite. Nevertheless, when students are asked to state the most essential single attribute in conducting, they usually list every other conceivable requirement but forget the most important. Therefore a few comments on this subject are warranted.

Leadership is both a long-range and a short-range matter. A conductor must develop in each of his performers:

1. A desire to belong to the group.
2. A pride of membership when accepted.
3. The willingness to practise the music on his own time and to keep his technique and himself in top shape.
4. The willingness to attend all rehearsals regularly and punctually, despite conflicts and inconveniences.
5. The willingness to work hard at rehearsals, and not just have a pleasant time running through the easy parts.
6. The desire to give the utmost, technically and emotionally, when the concert takes place.

It is impossible to teach how to achieve these objectives. Each de-

3

pends on the circumstances, such as the age and technical level of the group. Items one and two may be helped in the case of the New York Philharmonic by increasing the season to fifty-two weeks; with a junior high school chorus free soft drinks and a membership badge may work wonders. Everything must be done to increase the prestige of the group and its members; they must feel they were carefully selected and have a reputation to uphold. The group that has to rely on members who think they are doing the conductor a favor is incapable of a great performance. Conductors must spend much time pondering such problems. It is no use learning long lists of baroque ornaments if no one wants to play them under you.

At rehearsals, the conductor must show a judicious mixture of friendly persuasion, sternness, humor, patience, sympathetic understanding, praise, correction, emotional fervor, and occasionally a little touch of steel. An atmosphere that is continually namby-pamby can be soporific. Yet, on the other hand, few people will do their best if they are constantly being torn apart.

Most of the qualities of good leadership are the same, whether applied to coaching a team, running an organization, or conducting. Be fair; don't play favorites; give the newcomer a chance; be consistent in discipline; make the punishment fit the crime each and every time it is necessary; know your field; prepare your material; be willing to accept suggestions from the members; be willing to change your ideas when they do not work out; but, on the other hand, be positive. You are the boss; most musicians would rather be told to play something a certain way even if they do not particularly like it rather than be subjected to a constantly vacillating conductor. Working with committees is helpful, but eventually it may be necessary to remind them that the conductor is the one who is in the public view and takes the blame for what goes wrong. Therefore he must have the final say. Musical organizations are the last of the great dictatorships—benevolent dictatorships, we hope, but nevertheless dictatorships.

The modest young person who is not a natural leader may feel at this point, "I'd better give up . . . I'm sure to be a failure." Not so. If you are a good musician you can become a successful conductor by following these steps:

1. Study problems of leadership. Think about every group you have ever been in, musical or otherwise. Which leaders did you like? Why? Which ones were unsuccessful? Why? Can you list a few do's and don't's yourself? Why did you like your scoutmaster and hate your football coach? Attend every rehearsal you can, and talk to members of groups, musical and nonmusical. What qualities do they admire in their president? What is so good about a certain conductor? How did they like it when he did such-and-such at today's rehearsal?

Then apply these points to your conducting. You cannot imitate anyone else; you must be yourself. But you can apply basic rules.

2. Study as much as possible about music and related subjects in general and the score you are conducting in particular. This will increase the respect felt for you by the performers. While pedantry and a showing-off of knowledge are of course undesirable, command of your subject is vital. A musician soon senses whether or not he knows more about what you are supposed to be doing than you do, and reacts accordingly. Many a player has said about a conductor, "I don't like him much, but he certainly knows his stuff!"

3. Choose music you love. If you have a passionate desire to hear a certain piece performed a certain way, it somehow takes hold of you and makes you a better leader than you really are. Colorless and timid people often become incandescent when conducting, simply because they are transformed by the music. Sometimes we are required to conduct works we do not like; most of us are very lukewarm and insipid on such occasions.

4. Choose your proper work level. Some conductors do well with older people, while others are best with those their own age; some shine with talented performers, while others are ill at ease, being more effective with beginners. In the education field the conductor who was a failure at handling high school students in a rough district may be a success with junior high in a more intellectual neighborhood.

5. Take a personal interest in your players. They are people, not mobile instrument holders. Some need encouragement, others, criticism. A little consideration at a time of trouble is deeply appreciated. Suggesting to the second oboe that he leave the rehearsal

early so that he can visit his sick child before the hospital's visiting hours are over is not only the decent thing to do, but may also improve the morale and hence the playing of the entire woodwind section.

6. Develop a clear conducting technique. Musicians usually enjoy playing under someone who is easy to follow, and will forgive him for a multitude of shortcomings. On the other hand, when they are constantly trying to decode a succession of vague and confusing gesticulations they become highly dangerous.

A whole volume could be written on problems of leadership, group management, discipline, etc. However, most of it would be useless, as it usually depends on the exact details of the situation. If conductors constantly remind themselves of the enormous importance of these matters, follow the suggestions above, and use common sense, it will help more than long lists of Rules for Influencing People.

ASSIGNMENTS

Beginners:
1. Analyze all the leaders you have ever known.
2. Attend rehearsals of every possible type of group.
Professionals:
1. Ask yourself whether you are constantly aware of the importance of leadership.
2. Perform under other conductors as much as possible, to remind yourself what it is like.
3. Ask yourself whether you love the music you choose.
4. Consider whether you are sure you are working with the right type of group.

CHAPTER II

OTHER STUDIES

One of the faults of many conductors, young and old, is lack of background. They become preoccupied with the thrills and details of their concerts and forget that a vast amount of knowledge is required for good conducting. Their ignorance is often woefully apparent in their interpretations. Even many of our "name" conducting virtuosos show astonishing ignorance when performing older music, especially baroque.

Musical Subjects

The beginner must devote much more time to other musical subjects than to conducting itself. Harmony, counterpoint, ear training, score reading, analysis, music history and literature, orchestration, instrumental and vocal techniques are more important than baton technique. He should perfect his solo ability to a point where he can gain experience in interpretation through playing or singing solos and participating in chamber and larger groups.

The professional, in addition to reviewing and filling in gaps in his knowledge of the above subjects, should concentrate on two main fields:

1. Interpretation. This will be discussed in Chapter XX.

2. Music history and literature. The madrigalist should know not only his own area, for he will be a better conductor if he hears more classical chamber music or Wagnerian opera; the band man's ignorance of Bach's organ music and Brahms's piano works may account for a poor choice of tempos in band music; the choral person too often ignores symphonic music, and the pianist could learn much from opera.

This could be considered in great detail, but one illustration may indicate what is meant. In a performance of the Crucifixus from Bach's Mass in B minor, the conductor used a popular edition which indicated a number of crescendos and diminuendos. He followed these to an extreme extent. If he had any awareness of music history he would have known that neither the old *Bachgesellschaft* nor the *Neue Bach-Ausgabe* editions indicated any volume changes, and that such effects were virtually unknown in Bach's time. If he had heard more late Beethoven quartets, Wagner, Palestrina, and Gregorian plainsong, he would have realized by comparison that the effect he was producing was sensual to the point of lechery; he surely would have preferred something closer to the sublimity of the earlier church composers or Beethoven's slow movements rather than this *Tristan*-like orgy.

Innumerable other examples could be given. Northern New York is gently rolling; some of the natives think it hilly, but visitors from the Hudson Valley complain of the flatness. A transcontinental tourist knows that the hills are low compared with the Hudson Valley's, and very low compared with the Rockies, but that the country is not nearly as flat as Manitoba. The experienced traveler has perspective and a basis for comparison; the conductor must develop this in music by traveling through many styles of many centuries.

Non-musical Subjects

Educators and musicians have debated for generations the question of how much a musician should study in other fields. Languages are vital, and knowledge of the literature and art of many countries is something to be striven for. Parallels between architecture and music may help provide an understanding of the aesthetics of structure. Most musicians theorize about the physical aspects of sound, but few have studied the subject; a scientific background in acoustics would prevent many old wives' tales from being accepted. Even such unlikely subjects as meteorology and sports have been found of help. (Techniques for developing speed in plotting weather maps have been successfully applied to sight-reading; stamina drills, rehearsal schedules, and leadership techniques have been borrowed from track and hockey.)

On the other hand, there is an obvious limit to the amount of time a student can spend on non-musical subjects and still develop proficiency in his chosen field. One questions the value of courses in which the emphasis seems to be on memorizing insignificant details.

ASSIGNMENTS

Beginners:
1. Study all your other subjects.

Professionals:
1. Review basic musical subjects if they are rusty.
2. Study interpretation.
3. Hear as much music as possible.
4. Study art, architecture, literature, acoustics, etc.

CHAPTER III

CONDUCTING TECHNIQUE—GENERAL

Having touched on important fields of study outside the scope of this small book, we come to its main subject: conducting technique.

Many conductors fail to realize the importance of conducting technique itself. They accept sloppy entrances or choppy legatos, blaming the poor quality of their musicians, whereas the trouble probably is caused by their own right arms. They study scores before a rehearsal but never practise conducting; this is like a pianist analyzing a concerto and working out the fingerings but never playing it except with an orchestra. Conducting technique must be studied AND PRACTISED, during the entire career of the conductor.

Conducting is the most treacherous field in music. A soloist knows that the mistakes in a passage are his own fault and does something about it. Many conductors are totally oblivious of their own shortcomings.

In the field of music education, school groups frequently learn only four or five pieces a year. They polish them up to a high degree, and the performances may be quite satisfactory. However, the director fails to realize that they could learn more works and have a wider musical experience if they did not waste hours drilling details that could be perfected in much less time with a clearer technique.

A simple experiment usually convinces a skeptical group of the importance of a conductor. Ask them to sing or play the National Anthem pianissimo, molto legato, regardless of what you do. Start by conducting as well as you can; then change, contradicting with your arms your verbal instructions. Indicate forte, with harsh, angular accents, or dainty staccato, or a broad maestoso. The group will find it almost impossible to sing pp and legato when your actions are calling for something else, and the deterioration in the performance will be astonishing. When you return to conducting pp and legato the improvement is remarkable. (Of course, this assumes that the performers watch the conductor. Suggestions for developing this sensitivity are given in Chapter XXI.)

Choral vs. Instrumental

In the past there has been a lamentable tendency to split music into two categories, choral and instrumental. The choral man has usually been the weaker musician. He specialized in *a cappella* music, mostly second rate, and conducted every note he could manage. His scope of interpretation lay chiefly between barber shop and lushed up spirituals, with a dash of commercial radio. The orchestra and band men, however, were not exactly free from artistic sin either, much of it due to playing too many night club jobs and too few Bach cantatas.

In the United States today there is a strong reaction against such directors. It is realized that much of the world's great music is beyond their capability and understanding. There is an increasing number of dedicated musicians who are at home in both choral and instrumental music, and can conduct works for combined chorus and orchestra.

Many writers refer to the "choral style." Fortunately, the Great Masters never read such books. They treat the voice as another instrument, with words. To be sure, they consider technical limitations, such as range, volume, agility, etc., but they also do so with each instrument. The Benedictus from Mozart's "Coronation" Mass is really a string quartet for voices; the clarinet melody in the trio of the E Flat Symphony is a song. The Gloria of Beethoven's *Missa Solemnis* starts with the first five notes of the scale, played in double notes in the violins, reinforced in single notes by the wind; then it is stated by human instruments called altos and tenors, only now it has words; next it is given to trumpets. It is the same tune each time; voice and instruments are used idiomatically, but in the same general manner.

In the second movement of Stravinsky's *Symphonie de psaumes*, the flutes and oboes have a fugal exposition, based on an intricate subject which would be hard to sing; then the voices enter with another fugal exposition, only the new subject is more suited technically to the voice (or to horns or trombones or pedal timpani or any other less agile instrument); meanwhile, some instruments accompany the new subject with the old. There is no sudden change of style or of concept—merely of tone, the frequency of large leaps, and the addition of words.

This does not mean that the composers were not influenced by the text. The point is that the notes themselves were basically the same whether written for voices or instruments. Bach illustrates the crowing of the cock in the St. John Passion with a broken dominant 7th chord in the continuo; in the *Missa Solemnis* Beethoven symbolizes the Ascension with rising C major scales in the chorus; the music was influenced by the words, but the notes themselves were interchangeably vocal or instrumental.

Stockhausen and others even use vocal sounds at times purely for their color or rhythmical effect rather than the meaning—an *avant-garde* descendant of the Elizabethan's "fa la la" refrain.

Of course, there are cases when the rhythms and sometimes the pitches are determined solely by the sound of the words: *recitativo secco*, Anglican chant, and such passages as the start of the *Libera Me* in the Verdi Requiem. These are the exceptions rather than the rule.

To repeat: although there are many technical differences among string, woodwind, keyboard, brass, percussion, and vocal instruments, the Great Masters do not seem to have made a clear-cut difference between vocal and instrumental music.

Admittedly, the remarks above are arbitrary. But one concluding point is not. If a conductor uses the so-called "choral style" (beating every note), he and his choir have two grave limitations:

1. They cannot perform with instrumentalists, whose whole training has been to follow beat patterns.

2. They cannot perform music of a polyphonic nature. The conductor simply does not have enough arms to give every part its rhythm when each part is different.

The growing trend, therefore, is for all choral conductors to use "instrumental" technique: that is, to beat standard patterns, giving the beats instead of the notes, as described in this book. The writer is convinced that a good "orchestral technique" is superior to the wallowings of the "choral technique," and all the best choirs he has heard were conducted by directors using "orchestral technique." (Unbarred chants, as mentioned above, are exceptions and need special treatment.)

ASSIGNMENTS

Beginners:

1. Develop an orchestral technique and apply it to choral conducting.

Professionals:

1. If you are a choral conductor, be sure you use orchestral technique; work frequently with instrumentalists.

2. If you are an instrumental conductor, work with choirs as much as possible but don't change your technique. (Just remember that singers have to be given their starting pitches!)

.

Chapter IV

THE BATON

There are many myths about whether or not a conductor should use a baton. Consider these in turn:

1. A baton should be used for an instrumental group and not for a chorus.

    Why? Choirs have to perform biting, incisive rhythms, the same as a percussion section; violins have to sing smoothly, like a chorus. What is good or bad for one is surely the same for the other.

2. The baton gives a point to a beat.

    Wrong. Many baton men have no point to their beat, whereas it is possible to give a clear point without a baton.

3. A baton can be seen better than the hand.

    It depends. From the left side of the conductor, against a dark wall or suit, a white baton probably is seen better than the hand; from in front against a white shirt, probably not. Recently a guest conductor directed 400 performers in the Verdi Requiem, using a beige baton. After two or three rehearsals some performers were discussing his technique. An instrumentalist referred to the baton. Most of the chorus members present were surprised to learn that one had been used. From their places it was too far away to be seen.

4. A baton increases precision.

    It may, but not if it cannot be seen, or if it is so long it whips and bounces in a blur.

Leaving the realm of mythology, here are some further points which stand up better to logical examination:

1. A baton adds a length of rigidity to a beat which detracts from the flowing quality needed in a cantabile passage. Is it just coincidence that one of the greatest cantabile conductors, Stokowski, never uses a baton?

2. A baton magnifies any hand quiver to a conspicuous degree.

Most people's hands tremble slightly in a moment of tension, or even after strenuous movement. A baton announces this to all and sundry, making the conductor seem very nervous.

3. A baton robs the hand of an important function: indicating the mood by different positions. For example, a clenched fist for maestoso, a relaxed, flowing movement for cantabile, one finger outstretched for precision, the little finger raised for delicacy, etc. But this requires much skill and practice, and beginners should not be concerned with it. Therefore, all beginners should use a baton.

4. The baton, by enabling its user to shorten the distance his arm travels, reduces fatigue in a long or strenuous work.

HOLDING THE BATON

The writer was never comfortable with a baton until he changed to the grip advocated by Pierre Monteux—holding it as though you were shaking hands with someone, hands wrapped around the baton, the butt end against the heel of the palm. This seemed peculiar at first, but it gives much more control and provides for finesse, which other methods do not. The same grip is used on a fly swatter or hammer.

ASSIGNMENTS

Beginners:
   1. Buy a baton, preferably white, with a small cork handle. If the point is so long that it vibrates on a crisp down beat, chop it off. Practice swatting imaginary flies, using plenty of wrist action, and stopping short when the stick is horizontal and the forearm parallel to the floor.
Professionals:
   1. If you always use a baton, try the grip described above.
   2. Also try getting along without.
   3. If you never use a baton, buy one and try it.
   4. Batonless conductors—ask your friends whether your hand positions contribute to or detract from the mood of the music.
   5. Both sides . . . at the next few rehearsals you visit, see how well you can see the baton. Do you follow the stick or the hand that holds it?

Chapter V
ODDS AND ENDS

THE PODIUM

There is no point in developing a refined conducting technique and then not using a podium high enough for the performers to see you. The bottom of the beat is what counts, not your eyes. Be sure that when your arm is outstretched horizontal to the floor everyone can see it without straining. But beware of being so high that nearby instrumentalists are forced to look up at a sharp angle. If necessary, move them farther from you. This will also help you hear the whole group better. Keep your music stand almost horizontal and low enough to conduct above it. Ask your men whether they can all see you, and remind them to let you know any time your beat disappears.

POSTURE

As the performers cannot see what you do from the waist down but the audience can, confine all movements to above the waist. Keep your feet together and still. Every time you walk around you are a distraction, and the players take a fraction of a second longer to find you when they look up if you do not stay in the same place.

There is no excuse for bending, stooping, or knee bends. They may make the conductor feel that he is doing a great job, but they are merely distractions. Always maintain an attitude of alert watchfulness. Never look casual or indifferent as it is highly contagious. Make an exception if you want to relax the atmosphere in a tense moment.

MANNERISMS

Everyone sooner or later develops irritating mannerisms without realizing it. Once a young conductor marred an otherwise fine concert by constantly plunging his left hand into his pocket and rattling his keys. He asked for suggestions afterwards and was flabber-

15

gasted when told that he had just performed a concerto grosso for keys and orchestra.

Brushing hair off your forehead, scratching your ear—all these little habits must be eradicated like weeds whenever they appear. You cannot detect these peculiarities by yourself. You need a wife or a critical friend . . . or, at greater expense, a conducting teacher!

LEFT-HANDED PEOPLE

Most authorities agree that a left-handed person should conduct as though he were right-handed, with the right hand giving the beat and the left helping (as described in Chapter VIII). Otherwise it is very confusing to performers accustomed to a right-handed technique. Although a beginner may feel a trifle awkward at first, he will soon develop facility, and will have a decided advantage later when the left hand is added.

ASSIGNMENTS

Beginners:
1. Check this chapter frequently to make sure you are forming correct habits from the very first.

Professionals:
1. Ask your performers if they can see the bottom of your beat.
2. Tie your feet loosely together at a rehearsal and see if it bothers you. If it does, you are moving around too much.
3. Ask your wife or friend or son to check on other mannerisms.

CHAPTER VI

BEAT PATTERNS—THEORY

The next step in learning to conduct is to become thoroughly familiar with beat patterns. These are universally used by orchestral and many choral conductors and have evolved over a period of decades. They are based on the following principles:

1. The first beat of the bar must always be clearly distinguishable from the others.

The traditional strong beat is thus shown by the natural gesture of emphasis—downward motion. When we pound a table or stamp a foot to emphasize a point in an argument we strike downwards. Thus muscles combine with gravity. A sideways motion is muscles with no aid from gravity, and an upward motion is weaker, being muscles minus gravity. (Hammering a nail into a ceiling with a heavy hammer will prove this!) Of course, in many works it would be most unmusical to accent the first beat. Nevertheless, it is traditionally the point of harmonic emphasis and also the conductor's signpost. Showing it clearly is vital in helping the performers to count. Anyone can lose the bar line, but if the first beat, or "downbeat," is clear the player finds his place in an instant. If not, disaster may result. (In a well-known composition the performer may not need this help, but our technique must be based on the principle of making everything as easy as possible for the performers at all times.)

Even someone who cannot read music can quickly be taught to keep his place by watching the vertical beats and following the vertical lines on the page (the bar lines). This is the first step in teaching adults to read choral music.

This point is so important that an anecdote may be in order. In a rehearsal of a large chorus we sight-read the fast 2/4 section of the Confiteor of Bach's Mass in B minor. Afterwards the writer asked one of the best sight singers in the group how he had done.

"Not very well. I didn't have my glasses."

"But I thought you only needed them for distant vision."

"That's right. I couldn't see you, and I constantly lost the place because I didn't know where the downbeat was."

2. The theoretical secondary accents in a compound time signature are shown by motions larger than unaccented beats, usually made across the body.

Thus the accent on the fourth beat in 6/8 is shown by a large movement from left to right, with the other beats smaller. Obviously, as with the first beat, it would often be unmusical to make such an accent in the music, but these secondary accents are based on the theoretical divisions in the bar and are a help in counting. The conductor must be sure that the larger beats do not produce an unwanted effect in the performance; he can increase the size of the smaller beats and decrease the large to compensate if this is happening.

3. Give the beats, not the rhythms.

This is one of the hardest points of which to convince people. They feel an instinctive desire to put in the little notes between beats. Nevertheless, they must be told that extra, fussy motions on such notes happen too late to do any good and merely give the mind something extra to think about, thereby slowing down the tempo. Monteux, Koussevitzky, and many others have spoken strongly on this point. Experimentation shows that in most cases it is confusing and leads to sloppy playing or singing.

Proponents of extra motions claim that a beginner follows the hand, rather than calculates all the mathematical intricacies of the subdivision of the beat. This is false; untutored listeners have always kept time to music by beating the beats—that is, soldiers march in time to beats, not notes; folk dancers or just simple foot tappers follow the same principle. (Try marching to "Colonel Bogey" by taking a step on each NOTE instead of each beat!)

The conductor who gives beats instead of rhythms and lets the performers put in the notes between the beats is simply following the most basic principle of all music. There are a few cases when this rule should be broken, but most second-rate conductors break it far too often.

The basic principles stated above and the general outlines of beat patterns are widely accepted. However, the writer has a number of more or less original ideas which are applied in working out the details of the beat patterns given in the next chapter. These are:

1. It must be remembered that from the conducting viewpoint a beat is a *moment of time*, a split second infinitesimally small, like a point in geometry. It is NOT a duration. It marks the beginning of a period in time.

Thus "one" is like the starter's gun in a race; the next unit of time starts at the instant known as "two" and lasts until "three." A half note thus lasts from beat one until beat three. Therefore, the conductor must show each beat as an instant. This cannot be done by a vague, wandery motion; it must be a precise visual point.

The first beat is shown by a downward motion which is vertical and which "bounces" at the bottom. The instant in which it stops falling and starts to rise is the moment known as "one."

Try a series of downbeats. Hold the baton out in front of you, forearm and baton parallel to the floor, aiming directly in front of your shoulder; raise your hand up about twelve inches and let it fall to the same place, using some upper arm motion, some forearm, and a little wrist. When the arm is parallel to the floor let it bounce up again, almost of its own will. This is hard to describe but is a very easy natural act. The motion is like bouncing a golf ball on pavement. Your performers must be trained to play exactly at the bottom of the beat.

Try beating faster, with a vigorous hitting motion. Then try it more slowly, gently, like a large beach ball. But still it must bounce . . . a beat should *never* stick on the bottom or it cannot clearly indicate a point in time.

2. All beats should bounce at the same level.

Try this experiment. Ask a group of people to say "too," short and staccato when you indicate it. Hold your hand (with baton) out in front of you, forearm parallel to the floor. Raise your hand about twelve inches and bring it down, bouncing exactly where you started from. After a few tries they will all speak together at the bottom of the beat. Then start the same, but this time bounce close to the top of the beat; then go well below the starting place and bounce down there; then at some other level. They will come in raggedly, if at all. This illustrates two points:

a. Performers must know what you are going to do *before* you do it—they cannot really "follow"; they anticipate and perform *with* the conductor. The term "follow" is theoretically incorrect, as it implies being late.

b. If you constantly change the level at which your beat bounces, the performers cannot anticipate when you want them to play.

Imagine a flat surface like a table top in front of you, at a convenient height (usually elbow high). Call this the "bounce level." *Make all beats bounce at this level*, whether vertical or curving sideways.

3. A performer cannot see motion toward him with any degree of clarity.

The optics are simple: we follow sideways or up-and-down motion with large movements of our eyes as the object moves many degrees across our field of vision; motion which is directly toward or away from us is only visible through crossing or uncrossing our eyes, or by seeing the difference in size of the object. At a distance both these indications are minute. At an air show, a fighter aircraft coming directly at us at several hundred miles an hour does not appear to move, but merely hangs in space, with its wing span increasing and the color changing as the amount of haze between it and us decreases. A bicycle half a mile away going across our vision seems to be moving more quickly.

Therefore, *time should never be indicated by motion toward a player.* Do not use the type of beat patterns (so often shown in conducting textbooks) that make horizontal motions to the sides. While these are clear to people in front of the conductor, they aim directly at those on either side, such as violins or cellos in a symphony orchestra, clarinets in a band, choristers on curved risers, or practically everybody in an opera orchestra.

The problem then arises, if there is only one vertical beat in a bar, and no motions toward any performers, what about the other beats?

The solution goes back to high school geometry. Remember learning that a line touching an arc is called a tangent, and touches it at one point . . . an infinitesimally small place? Use an arc, touching the bounce level at one point only:

The above is for a legato, cantabile beat; a faster, more marcato style would have more angular points, as follows:

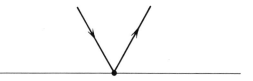

In bars containing many beats (e.g. 6, 9, etc.) some of the motions would be more like:

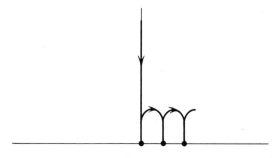

Thus performers everywhere will be able to see the exact moment of time the beat indicates and yet it will not be confused with "one," which should always be completely vertical, bouncing straight up a few inches before curving sideways. If it starts higher than all other beats it can never be confused with the others.

The beat patterns described in the next chapter have been evolved with all the above principles in mind. They are universally recognizable, and yet manage to avoid the errors of many variants frequently encountered.

ASSIGNMENTS

Beginners:

1. Be sure you understand and remember the principles stated in this chapter when developing your technique.

Professionals:

1. If you agree with the reasoning in this chapter, conduct for a few minutes and see if your normal technique violates any of

these principles. If so, mark them in the book and in the weeks ahead check back to see if you have cured the trouble.

2. If you disagree with some points, reread them, and then make a study of them when next you are performing under someone else. You may change your mind.

CHAPTER VII

BEAT PATTERNS—SPECIFIC

PRELIMINARY WARNINGS

1. The following are designed for cantabile, legato, mezzoforte, in a "moderato" tempo (metronome about 80 to the beat). This has been found a useful style with which to begin. *Modifications to all patterns will obviously be made for different tempos and characteristics* . . . shorter loops for faster tempo, more angular turns for marcato, etc., as described in Chapter IX.

2. Never stop at the bottom of any beat. Bounce, bounce, bounce! (For the reason, see Chapter VI.)

Beat Patterns (cant., leg., mf, moderato)

The first beat is in each case about one foot in length.

1 IN A BAR
Used in fast ⅜, ¾, ²⁄₄, etc.

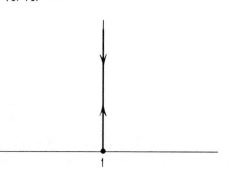

This consists of a continuous series of downbeats, all the same size unless the volume changes. It is used in a fast waltz, for example. (The diagram is of little help; imagine a ball bouncing repeatedly in the same place.)

2 IN A BAR
Used in moderate ²⁄₄, ⁶⁄₈, fast ⁴⁄₄, etc.

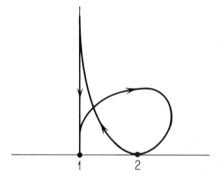

Note: As stated above, a fast, vigorous 2, as in a march, would be different, like this:

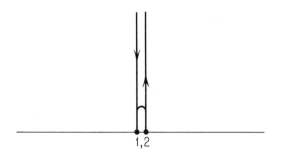

This is also hard to show in a diagram. 1 and 2 are in virtually the same place, but 1 bounces only two or three inches while 2 bounces up to the top again.

3 IN A BAR

Used in slow ⅜, moderate ¾, ³⁄₂, etc.

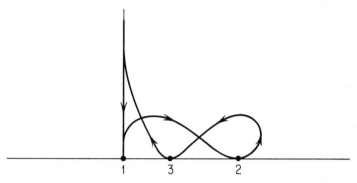

Note: Most people go to the right for 3, but this makes 3 so big it implies a crescendo, and also leads to an undue emphasis on 1. This also applies to the last beat in 4, 5, and 6.

4 IN A BAR

⁴⁄₄, ⁴⁄₂, slow ²⁄₄, ⁴⁄₈, etc.

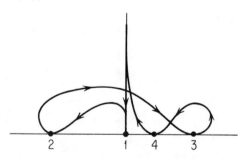

Note: The theoretical secondary accent on 3 is larger than beats 2 and 4, being across the body.

5 IN A BAR

⅝, slow ⅝, etc. (For fast ⅝, see Chapter XXIII.)

Look at 6 first, below, then study 5. Most 5's are split rhythmically into 2 followed by 3 beats or vice versa ("pure" 5's are astonishingly rare). This is indicated by the accentuation, chord changes, or sometimes dotted lines. As 5's are less common there is no standard method of beating them. Some conductors use a 2 followed by a 3 or vice versa, but this makes it impossible to distinguish the bar line.

It has been found better to use a 5 based on a 6, with the secondary accent across the body.

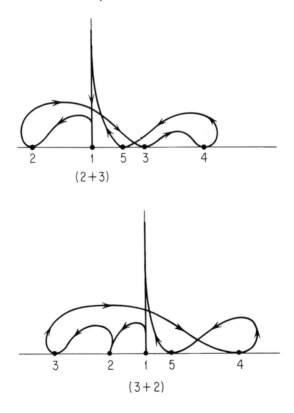

(2+3)

(3+2)

6 IN A BAR

slow ⁶⁄₈, some ⁶⁄₄'s, etc.

The pattern used by German conductors and most others is as follows:

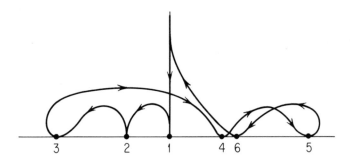

The French pattern violates several principles stated earlier, and in addition makes 5 and 6 much larger than 2 and 3, giving a feeling of crescendo in each bar. It is not recommended:

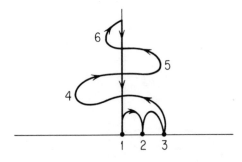

7 IN A BAR
¼, slow ⅞ (For fast ⅞, see Chapter XXIII.)

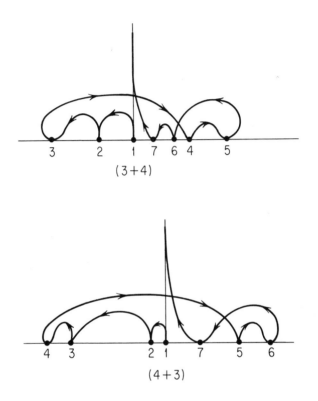

(3+4)

(4+3)

There is no general tradition with 7. Most 7's, like 5's, may be divided two different ways, with the strong beat on 4 or on 5. The above have been found successful. Like the 5's described above, they too are based on a 6.

Some passages in 7 are closely related to a divided 4 or an 8 (see below) with one beat missing, usually the last. Conduct as if in 8, but omit the appropriate beat.

Divided Beats

If any of the patterns above is used in a very slow tempo the arm moves so slowly as to be of no help to the performers. The conductor then gives twice as many beats (or three times, in the case of music in triple time). Thus a 4 becomes an 8 or a 12, etc. The principles to be followed are:

a. Preserve the original basic pattern.
b. Give additional bounces on the appropriate beats.
c. Modify the size of the extra beats in accordance with their musical importance.

This gives the following divided beats:

DIVIDED 1
Becomes a 2 or a 3

DIVIDED 2
Becomes a 4

Some theorists maintain that there is a difference between a slow ²⁄₄, beating eighth notes, and a slow ¼ beating quarters. They then specify using the following for a divided 2:

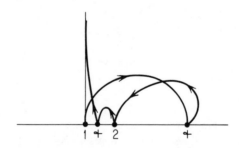

In practice, no justification for this can be found, it being a theorists' quibble. The Great Masters were quite happy writing adagio ²⁄₄'s or ¼'s indiscriminately. The author has never seen a celebrated conductor use a divided 2 for more than a few seconds at a time. It is an awkward beat and should receive a speedy burial, being exhumed only for brief intervals.

DIVIDED 3
slow ¾, ³⁄₂, some ⁶⁄₄'s, etc.
Do not confuse this with a 6; this is like a slow ³⁄₂ rather than a ⁶⁄₈.

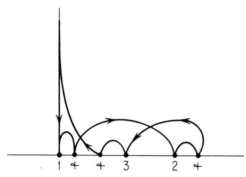

⁶⁄₄ may be either a 6 or a divided ³⁄₂. Even modern composers use it for both rhythms.

DIVIDED 4 (same as an 8)
slow ⁴⁄₄, ⁴⁄₂

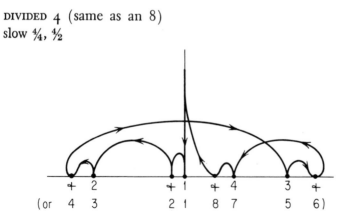

TRIPLY DIVIDED 3 (same as a 9)
¾, slow ⁹⁄₈

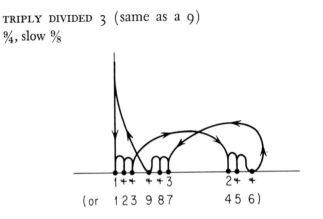

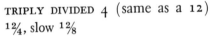

(or   1 23 9 87   4 5 6)

TRIPLY DIVIDED 4 (same as a 12)
12¾, slow ¹²⁄₈

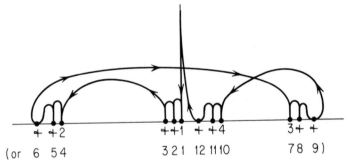

(or   6   5 4   3 2 1 12 11 10   78 9)

There will be cases in modern music where these equal divisions
will not apply. They can be worked out when the need arises, using
the principles given above. The problem of a changing unit of beat,
as when going from ¾ to ⅜, will be discussed in Chapter XXIII.

Further subdivisions may sometimes be needed (such as a divided 5 or 6, especially in a final retard). Follow the same principles: preserve the basic pattern and add little bounces to the

appropriate beats. Thus a gradually slowing 5 of the first type would be as follows:

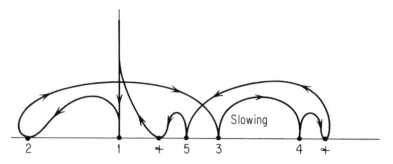

Subdivision will be discussed more fully in Chapter XV.

All the patterns above should be figured out and practised, a few minutes each. (Do not use the left hand at present.) If the professional finds he has been using different patterns he should decide whether his conform to the principles of optics and logic stated in Chapter VI. If not, he should seriously consider revising his own patterns. It is felt that clear patterns are among the most important assets any conductor can possess. If he differs in only a few cases and wants to change, he should spend more time on those until he is at home in them. It may take several weeks.

The beginner, on the other hand, should move ahead rapidly into the next paragraph, to be followed by the professional only when he is completely happy with his new patterns.

Changing Time Signatures

The beginner is urged to practise changing time signatures within a few minutes of learning the basic patterns. Most music of the twentieth century requires great facility in this technique. In training hundreds of young conductors it has been found that if they start working on this problem at the beginning of their career they never have trouble with it later, unlike those who spent the best years of their lives on Beethoven.

Try conducting the following meter changes (still cantabile, legato, mf, moderato):

$$\frac{4}{4} \quad \frac{3}{4} \quad \frac{4}{4} \quad \frac{2}{4} \quad \frac{1}{4} \quad \overset{(3+2)}{\frac{5}{4}} \quad \frac{12}{4} \quad \frac{4}{4} \quad \frac{6}{4} \quad \frac{9}{4} \quad \frac{12}{4} \quad \overset{*}{\frac{3}{2}} \quad \frac{8}{4} \quad \overset{(2+3)}{\frac{5}{4}} \quad \overset{(4+3)}{\frac{7}{4}}$$

* Beats keep the same tempo; this is a divided three.

Do it twice. Then do it backwards twice (for variety of order). Then do this:

$$\frac{2}{4} \quad \overset{(3+2)}{\frac{5}{4}} \quad \frac{12}{4} \quad \frac{3}{4} \quad \frac{1}{4} \quad \frac{4}{4} \quad \frac{4}{4} \quad \frac{4}{4} \quad \overset{(3+4)}{\frac{7}{4}} \quad \overset{(2+3)}{\frac{5}{4}} \quad \frac{2}{4} \quad \frac{8}{4} \quad \frac{4}{4} \quad \frac{9}{4} \quad \frac{6}{4} \quad \frac{3}{2}$$

Then do it backwards.

Do not conduct the exercises above more than a few times. You will soon half memorize them and will conduct the changes almost automatically. Thus you will not develop the technique of *reading* such meter changes in a new piece. Make up your own rows of numbers and conduct them. This will not only help you with modern music, but will also assist in learning the patterns themselves.

STRONG RECOMMENDATION

Find a flat surface such as a table which is elbow high. Conduct all the beat patterns, going through the correct motions and being sure you tap the table on each beat. (The surface, of course, represents the "bounce level" referred to before.) This develops an awareness of where your hand turns around and it keeps the bottom of all beats at the same level, a vital feature of the writer's system of conducting. Moreover, hearing your hand tap the table helps to test whether you are conducting in strict time. Many a conductor who can play like a metronome cannot indicate strict time with his beat because he is not completely aware of where and when his hand is bouncing. It also reminds you to "hit" each beat, firmly or gently, rather than to float aimlessly.

Do this frequently while practising the material in future chapters, and also throughout your career. The value of this drill cannot be stressed too highly.

WARNINGS

Several common faults make a beat hard to follow precisely.

1. Don't use a "hot stove beat." Many conductors give a slow downbeat and then flick their hand up quickly, as though they had accidently touched a hot stove. This leads to playing behind the beat and lack of precision. Many second-rate conductors have this fault, especially poorer band men, but the writer has never seen a conductor of the first rank with this characteristic. Keep thinking "hit . . . hit . . . hit . . . ," even if it is a very gentle hit.

2. Let the hand fall downwards with a constant and even speed; don't gradually "put the brakes on" toward the bottom of the beat. Performers, seeing the rapid fall at the beginning, naturally expect it to continue, and come in early; after a few times they are gun shy and play late.

3. Don't hesitate at the bottom! This stops the sense of movement. Bounce, bounce, bounce!

4. Keep the hand constantly moving. It should only stop at the very top of the beat, and then only for an instant, like a ball thrown straight up. (This is discussed more fully in Chapter IX.)

5. In all your conducting, be aware of the fact that your arm has weight. Beginners often move their arms gently through the air, as though writing lightly on a blackboard. If they pretend that their arm is very heavy, or else hold a stone or other weight in their hand, their beat will have more of the substantial character or "heft" it needs, and will also "bounce" better. This is hard to describe, but a conducting teacher can demonstrate it. The shoulder should always be relaxed, even with this weighty feeling.

ASSIGNMENTS

Beginners:

1. Study and practise all the patterns in this chapter, (cant., leg., mf, moderato), spending only a few minutes on each.

2. Almost immediately make up some changing time signatures and conduct them to develop this technique from the first. Don't stay long on any one set of numbers.

3. Then go back and work on the patterns again, until they be-

come automatic. Don't stay too long on any one pattern or you will find the next hard to learn.

4. Look in a mirror to see if you are doing them correctly.

5. Beat time while you or your friends sing a few well-known songs (legato, mf, moderato).

Professionals:

1. See if you agree or differ with the above patterns.

2. If you want to change, concentrate on those you want to adopt.

3. Try the changing time signatures. If you can do them slowly make up a few sets and try them allegro.

4. Look in a mirror. See if your patterns have the following faults:

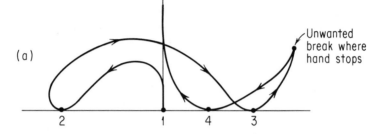

(a)

Unwanted break where hand stops

a. This gives a breath or phrase mark (or "comma") between beats 3 and 4. Bring the hand in smoothly unless you want to show a phrase. (See diagram for 4.)

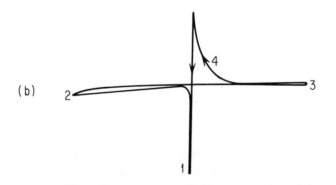

(b)

b. Too much emphasis on 1; also, the bounce level changes; also, the performers on the sides have trouble seeing the exact moment of beats 2 and 3.

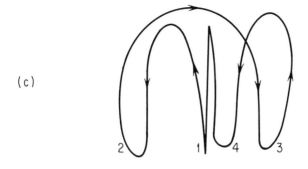

(c)

c. Performers on the sides cannot tell 1 from the other beats.

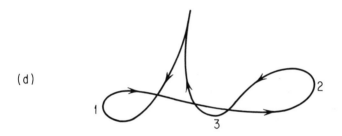

(d)

d. Where is the bottom of 1?

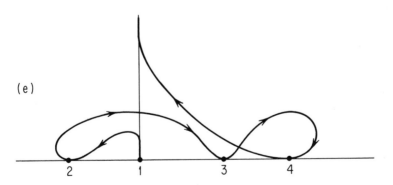

(e)

e. 4 too big; implies a crescendo on 4 and a heavy accent on 1.

(f)

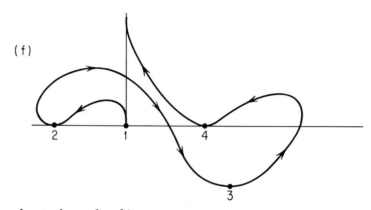

f. 3 too low and too big.

(g)

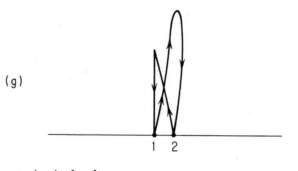

g. 2 is mistaken for 1.

CHAPTER VIII

THE LEFT HAND

There are many schools of thought concerning the proper function of the left hand. One is that "the right hand gives the tempo and the left the expression." If this is followed it means that all the performers on the right side of the conductor see an expressionless metronome.

Another is that it should be constantly extended, dancing in time to the music. This looks pretty but has no logical basis for its existence. The right hand, when properly trained, gives both the tempo and the character of the music, so why add something superfluous? Moreover, it often prevents those on the conductor's left from seeing the more important hand.

A third opinion was recently encountered: namely, that the left hand should duplicate the right, so that in a long piece if the right arm gets tired the left will be trained to carry on! This absurd idea is currently being taught in a graduate course in a major university.

The following practices are recommended.

1. Use the right hand for everything that it can conveniently show: tempo, volume, character, phrasing, and cues when they fit into the pattern (as discussed in Chapter X).

2. Use the left hand as follows:

a. To take care of duties beyond the scope of the right hand, such as cues that do not fit into the beat pattern, volume or balance indications to certain sections of the group, exhortations to supplement the right hand, such as an imploring gesture for a richer sound in a cantabile, page turns, and many other duties.

b. To reinforce and emphasize what the right hand is indicating. For example, add left hand for a sudden accent, a subito pp, the climax of a crescendo, an important cue, etc.

c. Under no circumstances allow the left hand merely to mirror the right for more than a few beats at a time. This is a common

37

fault. In a 3 pattern it is merely a waste of a good hand; in a 4, awkward, and in a 6, ludicrous.

d. When the left hand is not in use, either let it hang at the side or close to the body in a relaxed position, bent at the elbow. DO NOT LET IT CLUTTER UP THE VIEW. Many conductors park their left hands in mid-air and prevent the performers from seeing the more important right.

Thus the right hand should be able to conduct a concert reasonably well by itself, while the left hand maintains complete independence.

To develop this, the student should go back over the patterns in the last chapter and try to make his left hand perform a wide variety of actions while the right continues on its way. Set a metronome or play a record, beat time, and see how much you can do with your left hand without having the right vary the tempo or lose the pattern. Do things necessary to conducting, like turning pages and reinforcing downbeats, and also attempt numerous unmusical tasks like blowing your nose, arranging matches in a row, piling books on end, etc., simply to develop an automatic beat and an independent left hand. When this has been accomplished, as time goes on the left hand will take care of any necessary musical duties pretty much by itself, with a little supervision from its owner.

ASSIGNMENTS
Beginners:
1. Do a little of the above left hand drill each day. Don't be discouraged if you get mixed up at first. Start developing an independent left hand NOW.

Professionals:
1. Play a record, conduct from memory and watch yourself in a mirror. Does your left hand improve or detract from your conducting?
2. Try the same drill suggested for beginners. If you have trouble, get busy!

CHAPTER IX

DYNAMICS, ACCENTS, PHRASING, TEMPO, CHARACTER

When the student has spent several hours developing a clear, flowing beat in all patterns, practising mixed time signatures and gaining some independence of the left hand, he should proceed further. A beginner should not wait until he is absolutely perfect, but merely until his actions are semi-automatic. It takes years to become completely secure.

The beat thus far has always been cantabile, legato, mezzoforte, and moderato. Now other musical qualities will be discussed.

DYNAMICS

In general, dynamics are shown by the size of the beat. (See the previous chapter for the contribution of the left hand.) Try beating a moderato 4 as large as possible; make it quite absurd. Then shrink it down until it is controlled and not unseemly but still large. (If possible ask a friend to stand at a distance and give his opinion.) This is the largest you should ever beat, and you should only use this big a beat at the top of an intense crescendo. (With a baton, the hand will travel a shorter route than without.) Look in a mirror. Then look at your arm. Remember the approximate dimensions of this beat. It will differ from person to person. Someone with very long arms must use less relative motion than would a very tiny person or his beat will be ungainly and hard to follow.

Then beat time with as small a beat as possible. Gradually enlarge it until your friend says it can easily be seen by someone whose eyes are focused for short range and is taking a quick glance up from the music. (Here again, the conductor will move his hand less with a baton than without.) This is your pianissimo. Remember its size.

Now practise going suddenly from two bars of ff to two of pp and back (right hand only, for now). Then gradually increase from pp

39

to ff and back. Estimate where between these extremes you would beat for f, mf, mp, p.

Remember that you must show the performers what to do BE-FORE THEY DO IT. Indicate the sudden f just before it takes place . . . that is, give a large upbeat before the f, as though you were going to hit a fly you dislike intensely.

On the other hand, for a subito pp, do not let your beat bounce high just before the pp, or it implies a loud downbeat. A much whipped dog will shy if you suddenly raise a stick; likewise, good players will have trouble making a subito pp if your arm shoots up just beforehand.

Go through all beat patterns deciding the size limits in each case (still cantabile, legato, moderato).

Conduct the following:

If the last note worries you, read STOPS, page 72.

Jot down a few similar exercises and try them.

Test yourself as follows. Ask your friend to count out loud continuous beats in any time signature. Conduct him. See if you can make him follow your volume changes. Tell him not to be too cooperative; he must not read your mind but have you draw the effects out of him. If one person can easily follow you without music at a distance of fifteen yards you can rest assured that your dynamics will be clear to 400 singers and instrumentalists when they have the printed indications in front of them. If you cannot make yourself clear to him, work on it until you can. Go no further at present!

When you are certain that your right hand is capable of showing all dynamics, add left hand, here and there. Reinforce a crescendo, emphasize a continuous pp by making a "shhhh" sign in front of your lips, give a policeman's "stop sign" just before a subito pp, etc.

Two important rules about dynamics:

1. For continuous pp, keep the beat small. (Performers let a pp creep up if they see a beat expand.)

2. For continuous ff, on the other hand, do NOT keep the beat large. It flails and loses its effectiveness if used for more than a few beats. Ormandy whips the Philadelphia Orchestra through a tremendous crescendo to a furious ff and then reduces the size of his beat to about an inch, but it retains a hypnotic intensity while the ff continues.

ACCENTS

Accents are simply short volume changes, and should be conducted accordingly. (Off-beat accents will be discussed in Chapter XI.)

Conduct the following, being careful to show where the loud places are before you come to them (by making the previous beat bounce high). Don't bounce too high afterwards, to avoid implying a continuation of the loud notes (use right hand only).

Make up similar exercises.

Use left hand to reinforce the accents only when you are certain your right hand is showing them clearly.

Hunt up your long suffering friend (or wife or child or mother or conducting teacher) and ask him to count numbers. See if you can make him put in accents wherever you wish. Tell him he must shout out the accented counts only if you have virtually forced them from him.

PHRASING

It was mentioned in Chapter VII that stopping the hand in the middle of a flowing motion implies a breath or phrase mark. Up to this point the emphasis has been on developing a legato free from such breaks. Now practise stopping a beat slightly at the top to show the end of a phrase (without deviating from strict time). Conduct the following (right hand only):

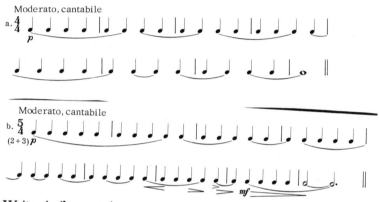

Write similar exercises.

Get your friend out again. Have him monotone "la la la" legato, with a slight break at the phrase ends.

Have him tell you whether:

1. Your phrasing is clear.

2. It is so overdone that it destroys the flow. This is hard—to show the phrasing clearly but subtly, without creating an uproar.

Check in the mirror to be sure that he is sufficiently critical.

TEMPO

For the most part this is simple and obvious. If the piece accelerates, beat time faster, and the converse. But all conductors should be reminded of a few treacherous points. A fast, large beat is unclear and frenetic; a small, slow beat moves too few inches per second to be of use. Therefore, the size of the beat should be influenced not only by the volume, but also to a certain extent by the tempo. BE SURE NOT TO USE TOO LARGE A BEAT IN A FAST TEMPO.

In an acceleration, or in a steady tempo when the performers are lagging, our normal instinct is to use larger motions; this merely adds to the weightiness of the beat and slows the tempo even more. Enlarging the beat is the way to hold back racing players or to indicate a slowing down, not a speeding up. Very few conductors realize this.

Remember:

1. When increasing the tempo or to make the performers catch up, make the beat smaller.

2. When slowing down or to hold people back, make the beat larger.

CHARACTER

So far, all beats have been legato, except where phrased. For different styles these are modified as follows:

Marcato. For a more energetic, marcato quality, hit harder, with more angular turns.

Staccato. Hit crisply, bounce the beat at sharp angles, but DO NOT LET THE HAND STAND STILL. When it stops for an appreciable time and then suddenly flicks to the next beat, the performers have lost the sense of time, and they cannot react quickly enough. If someone lobs a ball gently against a wall from a distance an observer can follow its path and anticipate exactly when it will strike; if the person stands motionless aiming a gun and suddenly pulls the trigger, the observer cannot possibly foretell the moment of the bullet's impact.

Many conductors do not know this, and in staccato music they stop their hands for most of the time between beats, with an untidy performance the result. The beat looks and feels staccato but is actually detrimental to precision.

A staccato 4 looks something like this:

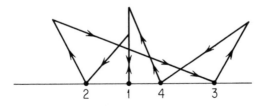

Maestoso. Heavy, ponderous movements are required. The downward motions should be slightly slower and weightier. For a legato maestoso, pretend you are pulling something very stiff but smooth, like pull taffy.

Slow, serene. This is the hardest of all. The mood of serenity must be projected, but the exact moment of beat must still be clear. It requires tremendous control of muscles and nerve. All motions must be slow and floating, almost hypnotic or trance-like, as in slow-motion films, but still retaining a faint trace of bounce at the exact moment of impact with the "bounce level."

Beginners should try this but not be discouraged if they lack the muscular control to do it properly. It will probably take several years to develop.

Advanced students should put a great deal of time on it to be sure they are clear and at the same time do not break the mood.

All music cannot possibly be categorized and described in such phrases as those used in this section. These are extreme examples. The cardinal rules are:

1. MAKE THE BEAT PROJECT THE CHARACTERISTICS OF THE MUSIC.
2. PRESERVE THE CLARITY.

ASSIGNMENTS

Beginners:

1. Conduct the following (right hand only):

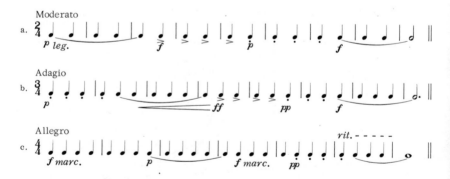

2. Review all the points in this chapter, writing or improvising new exercises, conducting a friend where possible.

3. Conduct one person (or several singing in unison) in well-known simple songs—community songs, hymns, etc. After some straightforward runs, change the dynamics, accents, phrasing, tempo, and character as much as possible throughout each song (without regard to artistry—this is a technical drill). See if two or more people can follow you, keeping together and correctly interpreting your indications. Ask them for suggestions.

Don't worry yet about starting or stopping. Give one preliminary beat, or several, or say "ready-sing." You have enough to worry about without considering the intricacies of starts and stops. Use right hand only, except occasionally to test the independence of the left. Do not do fermatas yet.

4. Play recordings of works in strict time with which you are quite familiar (e.g. Mozart's *Eine Kleine Nachtmusik*). Conduct from memory while watching yourself in a large mirror. Make sure that your beat is correct and that you show the changes in volume, etc. Never mind if you occasionally forget the music and make a mistake. The important thing at the moment is to do a lot of beating in different patterns, tempos, volumes, etc., while watching your reflection. Accurate score study will come later. But remember to SHOW WHEN CHANGES ARE ABOUT TO TAKE PLACE, rather than change just as the music changes.

Do several hours of this type of work before going ahead.

Professionals:

1. Try the exercises assigned to beginners.
2. Polish up any rusty spots they expose in your technique.
3. Test your ability to lead a friend through many changes, using right hand only. As an experienced conductor you are probably good at this, but you may find certain shortcomings, especially when time signatures are changing.

CHAPTER X

CUES

All the techniques up to now can be practised with only one person singing or playing. Now it is time to move into parts.

When one or more players have had rests while the music continues, it is frequently helpful to cue them when they start to play once more.

WHY CUE?

Cues accomplish the following:

1. Increase slightly the precision of the entrance.
2. Remind the performer of the character of the entrance.
3. Raise the performer's morale and thereby improve many other musical qualities (tone, balance, etc.).

CUES SHOULD NEVER BE USED TO SHOW A PERFORMER WHEN TO COME IN.

This point raises eyebrows whenever it is stated. Apparently many conductors allow their players to wait for cues. This courts disaster. *Every musician, instrumental or vocal, should count every rest in his entire life.*

Reasons for this are:

1. Cues often come too close together for the conductor to indicate.

2. Cues often apply to several widely separated players at the same moment: for example, the 1st flute, 1st bassoon, 3rd horn, and 1st violins. The second-rate conductor thinks he is doing a good job when he cues the top part, but this ignores the others.

3. Cues are hard to "aim" directionally. If the second sopranos and first basses sit next to each other and have adjacent entrances it is hard to give a cue to one section which may not be picked up by their neighbors.

4. The conductor often has more important duties than giving routine cues. Even if he cued a certain entrance in rehearsal, at the concert he may suddenly have to adjust the balance somewhere else, or hold back a section which has taken the bit in its teeth.

5. Cueing a player who does not know the place usually produces a late and poor entrance. The player should be secure and ready to come in with or without a cue.

At times a conductor should go through a rehearsal without giving any cues. This proves whether or not the performers are counting.

Why, then, give cues? As stated above, they help make a performer who is coming in anyway feel the moment of entrance a shade more precisely; it helps get him into the mood of the entrance (delicate, vigorous, smooth, etc.), and most important of all, it gives him increased confidence, shows that his part is important and that you are aware of it. *But he must be ready to come in anyway.*

Try this experiment. Ask a group of people to count 10 silently and on 11 to shout "Bang!" Give three or four beats to help them get started, then stand motionless. The shout will be ragged and feeble. Then repeat the process, only on 10 look up at them, giving an upbeat and a vigorous downbeat on 11. The difference will be spectacular. This is not a problem of counting, but one of timidity.

The same situation occurs when a nervous cymbal player has to hit a mighty crash after a quiet passage, and having counted 87 bars' rest, *thinks* he is in the right place. The choristers who suddenly shout "Barabbas" in the St. Matthew Passion also quail. They know when to come in, but a vigorous cue is a most welcome sight to one and all.

HOW TO CUE

Basically, a cue is like a start or an accent. One beat before, make an anticipatory gesture, and at the moment of entrance a decisive motion in a generally downwards direction, like "ready-go!" or "up-down!"

As with interpretative qualities, try to show as much as you can with your right hand (without distorting the beat pattern). Cues on the first beat to people in front of you are easy—look at them and put a little more emphasis on the beat, accompanied by possibly a rise and fall of head (and even eyebrows, but they are not really designed for cueing. Unless bushy, their range is small, and in a long work they can get very tired). Left hand may reinforce.

Other cues may fit in nicely; for example, in 4, a cue to people on your left on 2, or to your right on 3. In other cases the pattern would be destroyed. In 4 you cannot easily cue to your right on 2, or to your left on 3; in these situations the right hand maintains the beat and the left gives the cue, using an up-down motion as though it were starting a piece. Be careful when cueing to the right with your left hand not to collide with your right; sometimes a nod or a glance is preferable, together with more emphasis on the appropriate beat.

ALWAYS LOOK AT THE ENTERING PERFORMERS. Never cue with your head in the score. Look up, even if you never find the place again. Keep looking at them until the entrance is completed. Some conductors look away at the last minute in a manner which gives performers a let-down feeling.

WHEN TO CUE

All musically important entrances should be cued if at all possible. It may be a crashing tutti, like the first two chords of the "Eroica"; in this case you are cueing the whole orchestra. Or it may be a significant flute melody.

Also, you should cue entrances which are difficult for some reason or other—high notes for singers, entrances where the players have had innumerable rests, syncopated entrances (see next chapter), etc.

As for less significant places, the best rule is to cue if you have nothing more important to do. The second clarinet appreciates a glance or a nod when he enters to hold some unimportant note; he plays just a little better because of your attention; on the other hand you must not ignore an important crescendo in a 300-voice chorus simply to give an entrance to someone who was only out for two beats of rest.

WHEN NOT TO CUE

When entrances come thick and fast in all directions it is best to stop all cueing and simply give a good clear beat pattern. The performers can find the beats, whereas if you try to cue everything you look like a juggler and confuse everybody, including yourself.

You should establish a personal relationship with your brass players and be aware of whether they want a cue for important solos or prefer to be ignored. Many a brass player is so nervous that looking at him causes him to go to pieces completely. He wants everyone to pretend he isn't there, and this gets him through his solo. This is even the case with some first desk men in leading orchestras, and may have contributed to the growth of electronic music!

SCRAMBLED SEATING

This is the name given by the author to the choral seating plan in which the singers are arranged more or less by quartets. It was largely developed by Robert Shaw and has been adopted by some other conductors. (Those of us who have used it find it infinitely superior for tone, ensemble, balance, clarity, and sensitivity. Antiphonal effects are less satisfactory.)

When conducting a choir using this seating arrangement, cue as much as with a conventional plan, but make the motions in a general direction in front of you. The players watch for the cue at the proper time and see it easily, the performance being improved as described above.

ASSIGNMENTS

Beginners:

1. Practise cueing imaginary sections or single players in various locations in front of you on each beat of every time signature. Use left hand where advisable.
2. Increase your circle of friends to four and start conducting simple four-part choral music. Don't despise a lowly round to begin with.

Professionals:

1. Do you make your players count their entrances or do they depend on you? If the latter, you lead a dangerous life; resolve to change this at your next rehearsal.
2. Practise giving a few cues in unusual time signatures with various musical characteristics.

CHAPTER XI

OFF-BEAT CUES, ACCENTS, AND SYNCOPATIONS

When an entrance or accent occurs between beats it is often overconducted. MAKE ABSOLUTELY NO EXTRA MOTION at the exact moment of these notes; the worst thing you can do is subdivide (that is, put in an extra fractional beat or "hitch"). This action takes place too late to help and may slow the tempo. Conduct as though such entrances or accents were on the beat before (perhaps with a trifle more rebound than if *on* the beat).

Thus in a 4, a cue or accent on 3½ would be preceded by an anticipatory beat starting on 2 and a sharp stroke on 3, the same as if there were an entrance or accent on 3, although with slightly more rebound after 3:

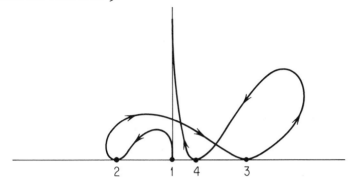

Remember the forbidden "hot stove" beat, referred to in Chapter VII, page 33? Here it may be used. Pretend that the "bounce level" was red hot when you touched it on 3, and bounce high with a snap.

If such accents or entrances should be gentle, remember to modify these actions so that they do not give an impression of roughness.

Conduct the following:

Allegro vivace

a. [musical notation]

Andante cantabile

b. [musical notation]

(Cues on the accented notes are conducted exactly the same as the above, only they would be directed at the proper section.)

SYNCOPATIONS

These examples are partly to illustrate off-beat cues and accents and partly an introduction to syncopation. It is universally agreed that in a syncopated passage the conductor should PRESERVE THE

BEAT AND LET THE PERFORMERS SYNCOPATE AROUND IT. They appreciate seeing clearly where the beat is so that they can play against it.

However, the conductor can help by giving crisp "hot stove" beats before each syncopated note. That is, the beat before the syncopated accent should rebound more than the others, as though you had burned your hand.

As with off-beat entrances and accents, DO NOT MAKE AN EXTRA MOTION BETWEEN BEATS.

Take example a. It will be conducted the same whether it is as shown above or is in this form:

On the other hand, for a long series of even syncopations, leave well enough alone. Conduct

as though it were

Note to professionals: There is one situation in which this rule may be violated. That is when everyone has a syncopation very close to the beat. It may prove better for the conductor in this case to conduct the syncopated note, adjusting the timing of his beats accordingly. The Crucifixus from Beethoven's *Missa Solemnis* is an example:

This is in a divided 3. It may be easier if the conductor gives the downbeat one 32nd note early, at the exact moment of the sf, elongating the next interval by one 32nd note to compensate. This is harder for him but easier for the players. Of course, they must have this explained or they will try to come in ahead of the downbeat, naturally assuming it to be the first beat of the next bar.

ASSIGNMENTS

Beginners:

1. Ask your friend to repeat "oom-pah" while you beat time in various patterns, giving a beat at each oom. Occasionally try to make him put a strong accent on pah, using your right hand only, without subdividing or varying the tempo. This requires a sharp rebound on the previous beat. Practise this with different tempos and degrees of accent.

2. Conduct (right hand only, the first time):

3. Find some examples of syncopations and entrances and practise them.

Professionals:

1. Try the assignments suggested above for beginners. You may find you are not as clear as you think.

2. Ask yourself whether you perhaps cause raggedness in your concerts by subdividing off-beat cues, entrances, or syncopations. Can you show them cleanly without subdividing?

3. Do syncopations bother you? If so, find a number of Brahms records and work on the syncopated passages. If you can keep straight in the syncopations of Brahms, the twentieth century can't fool you.

CHAPTER XII

CONDUCTING TO RECORDS

Many battles have been fought over the advisability of having students conduct to records. Those opposed claim that the conductor learns to follow rather than to lead. He feels he is doing a great job when Toscanini is really doing it.

While this danger admittedly exists, there are simply not enough opportunities for beginners to conduct. A great many hours must be spent moving the arms properly in order to develop a skillful technique. Beginners in tennis would never improve and champions would soon lose their form if they confined all their playing to tournaments. They must work against a wall or on a court with a friend, constantly practising their weak shots, as well as putting everything together in a game (tennis players need friends too).

By conducting to records, the student is freed from problems of rehearsal technique and nervousness, and is able to concentrate on arm actions. In a class the instructor can watch twenty-five people and give occasional individual suggestions adequately, with generalizations to the whole class when necessary. Each student receives twenty-five times more baton practice than if he were to conduct his classmates in live performance.

Three qualifications must be made, however:

1. It is assumed that conducting to records will be supplemented by live conducting as much as possible, especially as the student's technique and confidence grow.

2. The instructor must be sure that the student is correctly "anticipating"—that is, at a crashing sf entrance in the trumpets he must beat as though showing them in advance that they are about to come in, rather than being allowed suddenly to bounce high *as* the entrance is made.

3. The records should be mostly in strict time, like Beethoven symphonies. Obviously, the student can learn to set and change tempos, to stop, start, and conduct fermatas only with live music.

As for "following" a record, this is not completely bad, provided the conductor also learns to lead. In accompanying a soloist we frequently adjust our beat, and sometimes in concerts things go wrong and we must temporarily follow the group to avoid disaster. A conductor who cannot follow is almost as weak as one who cannot lead.

As a final point in the debate, it may be said that it is agreed that ability to conduct to records certainly does not indicate that the student can lead a live group, but surely, if he *cannot* conduct well to records he is not qualified to be in front of musicians or an audience. Too many experienced conductors cannot clearly perform the actions covered in this book and need to work a great deal to records.

ASSIGNMENTS

Beginners:

1. Select a symphony by Mozart, Haydn, or Beethoven (preferably one with very few fermatas, as these have not yet been studied; Mozart's G minor or Beethoven's Second are good choices). Buy the score and a record. If you have never worked on an orchestral score, you will have to read something about score reading and orchestral transpositions. Conduct the symphony, taking only a few bars each day and perfecting them. (Don't worry yet about fermatas and starts . . . let the record start and catch up to it. The important thing is for you to put in a lot of time developing correct arm action without the worries of starts and fermatas.) This may take at least two months, with occasional breaks to conduct some simple choral music live. If you go any faster you are probably not sufficiently self-critical.

Professionals:

1. Read the assignment for beginners, but choose a major work for chorus and orchestra, such as Beethoven's *Missa Solemnis*. Buy a full score using C clefs for sopranos, altos, and tenors and study the work in detail. Conduct to records, covering only a few bars at a time at first. Look in a mirror frequently. If any gesture seems short of perfection, practise it without the record fifteen or twenty times in succession, if necessary several days in a row. Each cue, each accent, each left hand motion must be dissected and reassembled. Only allow yourself the pleasure of a straight run when you feel the details are close to perfection.

2. When you have completed the above, try a modern score full of time signature changes, such as Stravinsky's *Le Sacre du printemps* or Walton's *Belshazzar's Feast* (but skip ahead to Chapter XXIII when you come to such problems as a ⅜ bar between two of ⁴⁄₄).

CHAPTER XIII

MORE ODDS AND ENDS

At this point enough material has been covered to enable the beginner to conduct records of classical symphonies, or other works in strict time. He must now put in many hours of practising so that his technique comes naturally rather than with a stilted artificiality. The professional must also do a good deal of work to assimilate completely any new ideas.

In addition to hints on practising, this chapter includes a few points which should be considered from time to time. They were omitted earlier to avoid giving too many instructions at once.

MIRRORS

Much practising should be done in front of a large mirror. If none is available the reflection in a window at night is almost as good. A violinist listens to his sound when working, and also to tapes if possible. The conductor, who works in silence, can only observe his technique in a mirror (or home movies or videotapes; these are excellent but expensive). There is nothing vain in such a procedure; you are actually benefiting your players and singers by seeing yourself as they see you.

On the other hand, do not use a mirror constantly or you will find it hard to do without.

SLOW MOTION

When a difficulty occurs in fast tempo, practise it in "slow motion." This is not the same as conducting a slow piece; you must do the exact motions you will eventually use, only moving very slowly, as in a slow-motion movie. This gives you time to think. You may even talk out loud to yourself to keep your thoughts straight: ("down . . . look left at the violins . . . raise the left hand . . . on 2 I must bounce the left hand in their direction . . . there . . . now look ahead . . . 3 . . . now look at the timpanist, left rear

. . . remember to cue him with the fourth beat . . . there . . ."
etc., etc.).

You should use a beat only as large as it will eventually be in fast
tempo, unlike a bona fide slow piece, where it would of course be
larger. When you can conduct the passage very slowly then try it
slightly faster. It may take several days before you can manage it to
your satisfaction at the concert tempo.

REVIEW

Take a few minutes to review the recommendation and warnings
at the end of Chapter VII, pp. 32-3. Beginners should now also read
the assignment for professionals on pp. 34-5 to make sure that they
are not developing those faults.

GIVE ALL THE BEATS

In certain places where the music stops moving, such as on a
held note or two or more consecutive rests, some conductors stop
beating entirely, on the ground that they should not make motions
when nothing is happening in the music. Many players find this
confusing; they lose the pulse, and the next note is ragged. In rehearsals they often stop playing altogether, thinking that the conductor is about to say something. It is better to keep the pulse going, using a very small beat; this cures the trouble without being
conspicuous. (This does not apply to fermatas, where of course the
pulse stops.)

Some conductors stop conducting completely for several bars at
a time in a concert. This usually scares the wits out of everyone.

WRIST

Be sure that you use a little wrist action but not too much. In a
fast staccato the beat might be only wrist; that is, the hand and
baton move and the forearm stays still. In a flowing beat made
by the whole arm a slight wrist action prevents having a rigid section all the way from the elbow to the tip of the baton.

Beware of using so much wrist that the effect is soft and floppy.

FACE

Facial expression is usually considered a vitally important part of leadership and musical interpretation. Some conducting teachers make their students conduct the class using face only, to combat the lifeless expressions often encountered.

It is felt that this is rather pointless. A student conductor is usually self-conscious and nervous, and this is the prime cause of deadpan conducting. To pick on him further and tell him to do something with his face simply aggravates the situation. When he has his own group, feels at home in front of them, and conducts music he loves, his face will have adequate animation.

Perhaps the writer is less concerned about face because of his admiration for Stokowski, whom he has watched from the front during several concerts. The maestro's face never moved a muscle, his expression never changed. The music was shaped just with his arms and hands.

GRIMACING

In moments of intensity, some conductors make wild facial grimaces. These are disturbing to the performers and actually make it difficult for a singer or wind player to keep his own jaw and neck properly relaxed. Beginners should guard against forming this habit. Professionals may find on inquiry that they are frequent offenders, or perhaps are only guilty during the intensity of a concert. The cure requires awareness and concentration.

SHOULDERS

Keep your shoulders down in a relaxed and normal position. When they creep up the effect is much the same as grimacing. Singers in particular may tense their shoulders in subconscious imitation.

MOUTH

Many choral conductors constantly mouth the words. This accomplishes little, and is ridiculous when the music is contrapuntal.

Such conductors usually mouth the top or entering voice, showing that they are not thinking the other parts.

The mouth is ill equipped to indicate precise signs at a distance. Why use lips for something which can be better done by the hand?

HAND POSITIONS

If you are conducting without a baton, ask yourself again whether your hand contributes to or detracts from the over-all mood. Does it show power in maestoso, grace in cantabile, precision, delicacy, or elegance where required? Does it change with the mood of the music? Or, on the other hand, is it clumsy, limp, or ugly? Does it ever contradict the mood, such as by making a mighty fist in a delicate passage?

The writer once had a graduate student whose thumb was very long and double-jointed. After a few seconds of conducting it would creep up and slowly bend back and point at its owner. There it would stay. The effect was mesmerizing. Nobody could pay any attention to the music. It seemed incurable until the student was persuaded to use a baton.

SINGING

Don't form the habit of singing when conducting; it is hard to break. You might contribute to a chorus (if you do not have a typical conductor's voice), but never to an orchestra or band, especially if you are near a microphone. By all means *feel* as though you are singing, but be silent. Beware even of grunts and gasps. They often spoil a performance.

Monteux once said, "Do not sing when you conduct. You cannot hear if you are singing."

MARKING THE SCORE

Beginners sometimes feel that there is something amateurish about putting marks in their scores. This is of course untrue. Even Stokowski keeps a large colored pencil handy and writes warnings to himself in huge letters.

A score is a maze of hieroglyphics, and frequently the most significant are quite small (for example, one tiny quarter note representing a monumental crash on the cymbals.) When the conductor is looking up and down frequently, as he should, it is easy to miss something important. Therefore he should mark such treacherous spots clearly in colored pencil, so that they may be seen at a glance.

In particular he should beware of passages where the same figure is repeated for several consecutive measures. The eye may easily lose the place, especially when the head is bobbing around, and therefore such bars should be numbered. Rather than relying on eyesight, the conductor then counts and is completely secure.

LOOKING UP

The importance of training the performers to look frequently at the conductor has been mentioned before. The conductor, on his part, must look at the performers almost constantly. Therefore, from the earliest stages of using a score he must train himself to look up at an imaginary orchestra, band, or chorus every few seconds. This is a special technique which must be learned, the same as arm motions, and it must be started early. *It is much worse to lose your rapport with the group than to lose your place.*

A FREE SYMPHONY ORCHESTRA

In the days before air travel it was difficult for a concert pianist to keep his fingers in shape when spending several days each week on a train. Many bought practice keyboards. These were not as good as concert grand pianos, but were better than not practising at all.

A conductor needs a symphony orchestra on which to practise. However, these are quite expensive, and therefore it is suggested that the reader equip himself with a practice symphony orchestra, band, and chorus. These are very cheap. All that is needed is a little imagination and a lack of self-consciousness. Go off by yourself somewhere and pretend you have the group of your choice in front of you. Visualize them in the set-up with which you are most familiar. Hold up your hands for silence. Wait for the oboe player to stop sucking his reed. Give an upbeat, and conduct. Go through all the motions you would if you really had your own private ensemble. In this way you can improve yourself enormously without paying union rates. When you finally have a chance to conduct, you are ready.

If you have your own group already you still need to practise away from them, especially before a concert.

This can be done with or without a mirror, and/or when tapping (as described on page 32). You can use records or conduct in silence.

CONDUCTING IN SILENCE

The more advanced students should practise an increasing amount in silence. This will develop the ability to keep the music going in their heads, and of course it is the only way they can practise setting or changing tempos, tempo rubato, fermatas, etc., without live performers.

It is surprising how few conductors practise in silence. When students are given final examinations in this manner, it shows whether they can set, maintain, and change a tempo, or whether they follow the performers. Also, preparing for such tests forces them to develop the habit of practising in silence.

THE METRONOME

Do not despise the lowly metronome. Many musicians are horrified at the thought of practising to one for fear their interpretation might become mechanical. In cases where strict time is desired, however, it helps greatly in developing the ability to maintain a steady tempo, and it is a ruthless critic.

On the other hand, be cautious of metronome settings when choosing the tempo of a piece. Many metronomes are inaccurate, including electric models, which sometimes have a chronic error of as much as 30 or 40 per cent and may be further affected by a change in line voltage. Set yours to 60 and count how many ticks it makes in one minute. It should, of course, be 60. Even if the markings are the composer's own and not an editor's wild guess, few composers check theirs or know that errors may exist. (Brahms is reported to have said in his later years that he strongly disagreed with many of the metronome markings that he had put on his earlier works.) Fortunately, most of them tick evenly. Pocket metronomes are the most convenient, although they too are sometimes incorrect.

Once you find a metronome which is ticking evenly, set it to a tempo that seems right for the piece you are working on, and conduct. You may be appalled at how the ticks seem to run ahead or drag.

At L'École Monteux, one of the writer's colleagues had occasion to visit the great old man at his house. When the student went in, "Maître" was sitting with the score of a classical symphony in front of him, conducting a ticking metronome. If this renowned artist felt he needed such practice, let no lesser man scorn it.

PITCH

Pitch in choral singing can sometimes be altered somewhat by conducting technique. Flatting may be reduced by beating with a lifting action, or by gradually raising the left hand. Sharping as well as flatting may be reduced by pointing downwards or upwards respectively to warn the singers of the trend. These are last minute devices, however, and if used too much will become ineffective. Many factors are involved in choral intonation, a complicated subject beyond the scope of this book.

FRILLS

Be sure that everything you do has a purpose, and that it has a specific effect on the music. Otherwise eliminate it. The players see your arms flapping around enough as it is, without having the scene cluttered with meaningless frills. For example, one teacher used to require his students to turn their hand to the right on the 3rd beat of a 4 bar. He had no reason other than to "make it look nice." As this has no musical effect, it is a frill and should be avoided. Likewise, guard against extra loops and waggles which are not called for in the music.

INDIVIDUAL STYLE

Does this mean that the conductor should not develop his own personal style? In a sense, yes. A conscious effort to be distinctive will look artificial. You will be distinctive naturally from the moment you start studying conducting even if you rigidly follow everything in this book. Your arms, hands, and face are your own and will always have your own personal qualities. When a class of twenty-five beginners are all shown the same beat and then attempt to duplicate it they remain twenty-five highly different individuals . . . sometimes too much so!

The best way to become distinctive is to develop a conducting technique which is clear and totally subservient to the needs of the music. This will mark you as a rarity among conductors.

ASSIGNMENTS

Beginners:

1. Every few days re-read one of the earlier chapters. See if you are forgetting anything. If so, mark it in the book and check up on yourself again in a few weeks.

Professionals:

1. A little review wouldn't hurt you either.

CHAPTER XIV

STARTS AND STOPS

Considerable time should be spent on the previous chapters before attempting the nerve-racking problems of stops and starts. The instructor must be particularly sure that a timid beginner has reasonable command over the earlier material before being plagued with this.

In all starts the conductor's motions must indicate the following:

1. the exact moment at which the piece is to commence
2. tempo
3. mood (volume, etc.).

Far too many conductors and even books only consider the first.

There are two starting situations: A: pieces which start on a beat, and B: those which start between beats.

A. *Pieces Which Start on a Beat*

1. Stand still, baton out in front at the "bounce level." Make sure all performers are ready and attentive. (With singers be sure they have been given their note.)

2. Give the beat immediately ahead of the one on which the piece commences. That is, if it is in ¾ time and starts on 3, give 2; if on 1, give 3, etc. This beat must be anticipatory in character, and facial expression, shoulders, etc., must contribute to this feeling. Left hand may also be used.

3. The starting beat itself then is given, with as much emphasis and confidence as the mood of the piece permits.

Note: a. The preliminary beat must start EXACTLY one beat before the piece is to commence; otherwise it will not indicate the tempo. Those conductors who habitually give a quick preliminary beat fail their performers in this important respect—especially important when a new section commences in a different tempo after only a brief pause.

b. The preliminary beat, while borrowed from the basic beat pattern, is modified somewhat. If the piece starts on 1, raise the baton directly from the "bounce level" . . . do NOT go down first. This habit can increase until half your performers mistake the downwards motion for the downbeat itself, as has happened with many guest conductors. An upbeat at the start goes *up*. That way ↑!

Other preliminary beats will start up and come down, but in a diagonal direction. Thus starting on 3 in a three pattern:

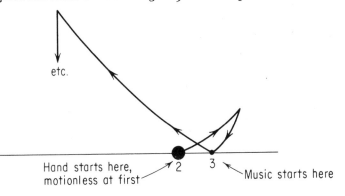

etc.

Hand starts here, motionless at first   2   3   Music starts here

If a piece starts on 2, with no rest ahead of it, the procedure is different. Hold the baton at the top of a small 1, then drop it down and bounce it up from the "bounce level," with a "dead pan" expression to prevent people from coming in early. The left hand will help if held out stationary. Then move vigorously and confidently into 2, mirroring with your left hand, and the piece commences. This is always difficult and needs practice with the performers. Nevertheless, if you do it clearly they will follow easily after one or two attempts, if not the first time. This is illustrated as follows:

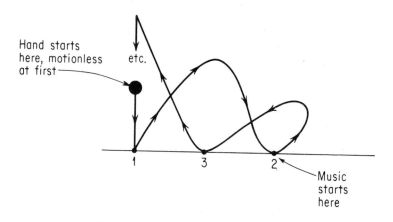

The same principle applies when conducting 1 to a bar. Start high, go down, bounce higher; on the next beat the music starts.

CHARACTER OF THE PRELIMINARY BEAT

The preliminary beat must also indicate the character of the piece . . . vigorous, languorous, delicate, majestic, etc.

DO NOT BECOME SO WORRIED ABOUT STARTING A QUIET PIECE THAT YOU MAKE IT SOUND STRAINED AND AGITATED.

DO NOT BE SO CONSCIOUS OF MAINTAINING THE MOOD IN A QUIET PIECE THAT YOU ARE TOO VAGUE AND IT DOESN'T START AT ALL.

Starts are among the most neglected features of conducting and they require a tremendous amount of practice.

ASSIGNMENTS

Beginners:

1. Don't despair at all this. After a few tries it will come more easily. Get two people and make them follow a number of starts. Commence with simple songs starting on 1, then take a few starting on the last beat of the bar. Try several tempos, dynamic levels, and moods. Only when you feel quite confident should you try pieces starting on other beats, especially on 2.

Professionals:

1. If you are convinced your starts are crystal clear, conforming to all requirements, see if you can do the following:

If you have any hesitation whatsoever in starting these, you need more work. The point is not that in a concert there are so many starts, but in a rehearsal you are continually starting in the middle of a piece, and rarely in places which can be practised in advance.

B. Pieces Which Start Between Beats

Such a start as

$$\frac{3}{4} \, \flat \, | \, \textstyle \rule{0pt}{1em} \quad \rule{0pt}{1em} \quad \rule{0pt}{1em} \, |$$

is difficult, and authorities split three ways on how to do it.

One school of thought says to subdivide and beat the eighth note. This is the refuge of the destitute; it produces a flustered motion and occurs too late to help. If the first note were a sixteenth it would be impossible.

The next group simply gives the upbeat and lets the performers come in where they may, halfway through it. Although this practice is widespread, it violates logic. The conductor is actually asking the players to come in halfway through a unit of time *before the unit has been defined*. If they manage to guess right all is well; otherwise the start is usually insecure.

Take a visual analogy. Suppose you are watching a man walking beside a fence. Part way along he stops and marks it with a vertical chalk line. Then he asks you to tell him when he is halfway to the next line (which has not yet been marked), and he starts walking again. You are puzzled, then you realize he has asked the impossible. But suppose he puts *two* lines on the fence, a few feet apart. After the second he asks you to stop him halfway to the next. You look back and easily estimate the halfway point.

The significance is this: you were unable to help him the first time because the unit had not been established, and therefore you could not estimate the half unit; the second time it was easy.

Therefore, in the musical example above it is strongly recommended that you join the third school of thought: give 2 and then 3; this establishes the time interval between beats, and the musicians can estimate the fraction, as follows:

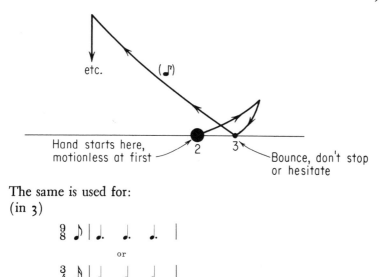

The same is used for:
(in 3)

In one case they estimate two-thirds, and the other three-quarters of a beat. Otherwise the tempo cannot be shown, merely the moment of commencement.

To put this in a rule:—FOR STARTS BETWEEN BEATS, GIVE TWO BEATS BEFORE THE FIRST NOTE.

The writer taught this method for several years and was encouraged later to find that Pierre Monteux insisted on it.

However, there is one danger. Performers who are accustomed to coming in after one beat may misinterpret the first motion and come in too soon. Therefore, the first beat must be given very casually, small, with left hand held out motionless. Then the next beat will be larger, with more snap, and a real feeling of "this is the one that counts"; then the left hand will make some decisive motion too. NEVER make an extra motion at the exact moment when the first note should be played in type B starts. This slows you down and makes good players nervous. It is quite unnecessary if you have a clear technique. AND NEVER STOP AT THE BOTTOM. It destroys the sense of flow. Bounce, bounce, bounce!

EXCEPTION TO THE RULE

Some pieces start with a very short note before a long first beat:

Beethoven Symphony No. 2
Adagio molto

Monteux advocated one upbeat, with the first note on the down-beat, as though it were

This works wonders with such a start. (A few bars later, where the same figure occurs in strict time, it must, of course, be played literally, as written.)

Further Points About Starts

EXTRA PRELIMINARY BEATS

In some cases it may be practical to give several preliminary beats, if you have time. But you and your group must develop the technique of starting with only one (or, in type B, two), for those cases where the music does not allow time for extra beats.

At Tanglewood we had a lengthy discussion on how to start the scherzo of the "Eroica," which you will remember is in a fast ¾ conducted in one, with a quarter note anacrusis. Some said to give one beat, others two. We decided to watch and see how Koussevitzky started the Boston Symphony Orchestra that night in a concert. He gave FOUR full bars, and at the same time showed the counts with his mouth! The start was miraculous and to the uninitiated sounded effortless. However, this would obviously be out of the question at the start of the allegro of the last movement of Beethoven's First Symphony, where there cannot be a long gap after the fermata which concludes the slow introduction.

AFTER YOU, ALPHONSE

Timid conductors often hesitate just as the music should commence. They are afraid the performers will come in late. Seeing this, the musicians wait for the conductor, who in turn hesitates further. Soon it is a case of "after you, Alphonse." NEVER HESITATE WHEN CONDUCTING A START. Act rhythmically and with confidence. If the players are late, stop and make them start *with* you. Soon they will form this good habit. But if they know you regularly hesitate, they will never come in on time.

MYSTIC SYMBOLS

For some mysterious reason, many students unknowingly make a series of small movements in mid-air with their hand before starting a piece. These puzzle the performers and are sometimes mistaken for preliminary beats. Avoid such mystic symbols. It is surprising how hard they are to suppress.

PRELIMINARY RESTS

A composition in ¾ starting on 2 may be written

♩ ♩ |♩ ♩ ♩ |

or

|♩ ♩ ♩ |♩ ♩ ♩ |

If there are rests before the sound commences, the piece must be considered to *start with the rest*, so the conductor must give a small preliminary beat before the rest and another on the rest, with a large rebound. Otherwise a player with only an instrumental part in front of him may miscount. With a chorus this precaution may not be necessary unless they are singing from parts.

"MERGING" AFTER A START

Certain awkward beginnings are facilitated by starting with more beats per bar than the piece requires, and then "merging" (the opposite of subdividing), as described in Chapter XV.

For example:

Be sure the eighth note beats are not so large and fast as to be flustered.

LAST WORD ON STARTS

When all is said and done, there are two cardinal rules about starts which must dominate all others.

1. A START MUST LOOK LIKE A START.

   This sounds ridiculous, but a student often goes through all the correct motions and the piece does not begin. This is because he somehow failed to make the start look like a start. It is hard to teach or describe. Everything must contribute . . . face, eyebrows, perhaps mouth, breathing action, shoulders, and exact nature of the arm movements. This comes with practice and perhaps a certain innate sense of pantomime.

2. NOTHING BEFORE THE START MUST LOOK LIKE A START.

   There must be no mystic symbols, twitches, or other confusing motions; in particular, in Type B starts be sure not to let the first motion look like the more important second and final preliminary.

Stops

It should be easy to stop a piece, but many people make a difficulty of it.

A final bar may have a whole note for the strings, four quarters for the horns, a bass drum stroke on the third beat and a cymbal crash on the fourth. Obviously each beat must be given. The strings have no way of knowing when this situation arises. Therefore, on a final note, they are trained to watch for all the beats, to avoid cutting off too soon. Hence it is best in a new piece to give all the beats (small) in the last bar even where nothing new is happening. However, once the players become familiar with a composition this seems pedantic. Most conductors give 1, then hold it as long as they wish and cut off.

But the problem is, how to cut off. Notes do not just end, they must be stopped. The timpanist has to stop his stick on the way down; singers usually have to add a final consonant. Where the length of the final note is optional, as at a final retard or a fermata, the conductor must show in advance that he is about to cut off. He cannot simply drop his hand. Many complex and ineffective ways to do this are being taught. Some people use a written "e" for no apparent reason; others make wild swoops in several directions, and nobody knows exactly when to stop. The simplest way is the best: hold still, then give two short motions, one up, the other down, returning to exactly where it started from . . . up, down, like "ready, go!" (For a more flamboyant occasion like the last note of *Die Meistersinger*, a larger beat could be used!) But the principle is simple: prepare, cut.

ASSIGNMENTS
Beginners:
1. Conduct:

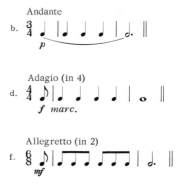

Tempo di Valse (in 1)

g.

mp leg.

Moderato (in 6)

h.

f marc.

Lento

i.

ff

Allegro non troppo

j.

p leg.

Allegro vivace (in 4)

k.

f

Andante con moto

l.

p poco marc.

Allegretto grazioso (in 3)

m.

p leg.

Largo (in 4)

n.

p leg.

2. Practise every possible start in every beat pattern, at widely varied tempos and volumes, first type B, then a mixture of A and B.

3. Put your two friends far apart in a room with a blackboard. Write a number of exercises similar to those shown in this chapter on the board and see if you can make your friends

start together *without telling them the tempo or character in advance*. An hour or two of this will work wonders with a subject which is difficult to read about.

4. From now on, at the conclusion of each exercise concentrate on making a clear cut-off.

Professionals:

1. Conduct:

Allegro vivace (in 3)

a.

Moderato

b.

Andante

c.

Presto (in 1)   Andante espressivo

d.   e.

Maestoso   Moderato

f.   g.

Allegro molto

h.

Allegro molto

i.

Andante

j.

2. Give yourself further practice as indicated for beginners, placing more emphasis on unusual situations (such as ⅝ time).

3. With your two friends, concentrate especially on conveying the mood without their knowing in advance what it will be. They should know the tempo, volume, and mood BEFORE YOU HAVE REACHED THE BOTTOM OF THE STARTING BEAT. Most conductors lack this capability because they never work on it as a separate drill.

4. Think about your cut-offs and see if they need tidying up.

CHAPTER XV

SUBDIVISION AND "MERGING"

The term "subdivision" (or less frequently "division") is commonly used to indicate a conductor's action when he changes the beating unit to a lower note value; for example, when he goes from quarter notes to eighths, giving 8 beats in a bar where formerly there were 4. "Merging" is the author's term for the opposite, which seems to have no generally accepted name.

A: Subdivision and Merging Within a Piece

Subdivide or merge only if the tempo is changing. In other circumstances this usually implies a tempo change and therefore induces one inadvertently. Monteux was very strict in forbidding subdivision or merging in strict time.

Subdivision is advisable when the tempo is slowing down to the point where the beat becomes unwieldy. This is common at a final retard. The conductor gradually slows his beat and at a certain point starts putting in the extra bounces described in Chapter VII, being careful to preserve the skeleton of the basic pattern. He may divide anywhere within a bar, but once divided he must stay divided until the tempo picks up.

Three bars of a final retard might be conducted as follows:

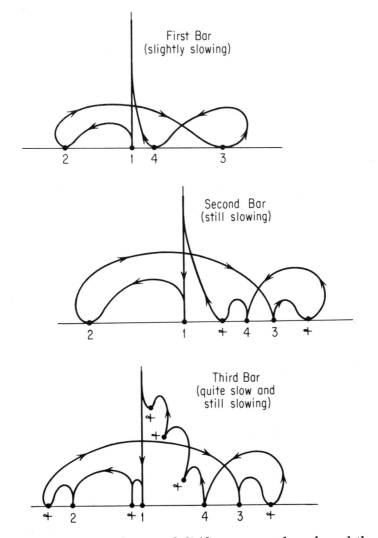

First Bar
(slightly slowing)

Second Bar
(still slowing)

Third Bar
(quite slow and
still slowing)

The first is in 4, the second divides part way through, and the last is all divided. In an extreme case the beat might even be doubly divided, as the last diagram shows. But notice that THE BASIC PATTERN IS CLEARLY PRESERVED. We must not wander all over.

Sometimes it is helpful to subdivide just before the actual slowing down occurs. With a strange orchestra and little rehearsal time this warns of the coming retard and is more clearly seen than simply slowing the beat.

It should be remembered that although there are many degrees of final retardation, in most cases a GRADUAL slowing down is expected, with the beats becoming progressively farther apart. There should be no sudden change into a slow section which then continues in strict time, and of course no acceleration. One rarely hears an amateur do a well-proportioned final retard; there are lumps and bumps and great holes where nothing happens, especially at the exact moment of subdivision, where the tempo often suddenly changes. Such retards sound like:

• • • • • • • •   •   •   •   •

     or

• • • • • • • •   •   •   •   •

Try to make final retards like

• • • • • • • • • • •   •   •

     or

• • • • • • • • • •   •   •   •   •

(Of course, if there is a sudden adagio, that is a different matter.)

Merging is less common. Sometimes in an acceleration the beats would be too fast to be clear; the conductor then merges two or three beats together and continues thus in the faster tempo. For example, in a Strauss waltz he may start in 3, and gradually accelerate. When the beats are in danger of becoming too fast he merges them and conducts 1 in a bar.

In the writer's youth he had great trouble making his orchestra accelerate sufficiently in a Strauss waltz when he stayed in a fast 3; then he tried merging into 1, part way through the acceleration, and the trouble was instantly cured—a fine illustration of bad conducting rather than bad performers.

MERGING AFTER A START
See the use of merging described earlier in Chapter XIV.

ASSIGNMENTS
Beginners:
1. Conduct:

2. Have a friend count beats in various time signatures while you conduct retards and accelerations extreme enough to warrant subdividing or merging. Practise subdivision, starting on each beat of every pattern.

Professionals:

1. Conduct the following exercises. Do each several times, increasing the amount of retard progressively, subdividing one beat earlier each time.

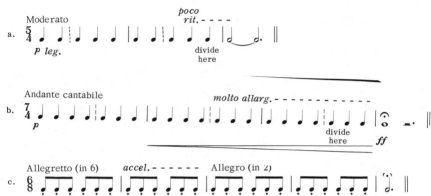

2. Test yourself on other uncommon time signatures. Be sure that your retards are well proportioned.

B: Subdivision and Merging for an Entire Piece

In many pieces there is no doubt how many beats to give in a bar. A 2/4 march could be nothing but 2; 1 would be absurdly slow and 4 ridiculous. The Hallelujah Chorus from *Messiah* could only be in 4, even if taken unusually quickly or slowly; 2 would be uncontrolled and 8 frantic.

However, a great many compositions are performed at a tempo where the choice for the conductor is by no means clear cut. For example, the well-known tune in the last movement of the Brahms First Symphony might be taken in a rather fast 4 or a rather slow 2; the third movement of Mozart's G minor could be in a fast 3 or a slow 1; *My Bonnie Lies Over the Ocean* and *Drink to Me Only with Thine Eyes* might be in a fast 6 or a slow 2.

It must be emphasized that THE TIME SIGNATURE IS OF LITTLE HELP. The symbols C and ¢ were used indiscriminately up until about 1800; in Beethoven's *Missa Solemnis* there is unmistakable evidence implying that C means 4 to a bar and ¢ means 2 (the "et resurrexit" section), but this is nineteenth-century habit.

Some modern composers use ²⁄₂ when they want two beats to a bar and ⁴⁄₄ for four. But composers are not necessarily the best judges of how to conduct their own music even if their musical instincts are infallible.

How, then, does a conductor determine in such cases whether to use more beats in a bar (by subdividing a ⁴⁄₄ and conducting in 8, etc.) or fewer beats (such as a ⁴⁄₄ in 2)?

He should first settle in his mind the tempo and character of the piece, or of its principal sections, whether it should be flowing or sturdy, four vigorous accents per bar or two gentle ones, etc. Then he makes his choice according to the following table:

Using MORE beats in a bar:	Using FEWER beats in a bar:
1. gives a sturdier motion	1. gives a more flowing motion
2. may facilitate certain accents or entrances	2. may make certain accents or entrances harder
3. tends to keep a tempo slower	3. tends to let a tempo move faster

Go back to the four examples mentioned earlier. Sing each one. Conduct a group singing them if you can. Try each tune both ways (e.g. the Brahms in 4 and in 2). Change every two or three phrases from one to the other. You will soon feel the difference. It is truly remarkable. The performers need know nothing of what you are doing. It seems to be a universal and instinctive matter not related to musical instruction.

If you want the Brahms and the Mozart to flow along, you must conduct in 2 and 1 respectively; if you want a sturdier effect (as is probably more desirable in these cases) you must use 4 and 3. *My Bonnie* becomes jerky and choppy in 6; the ocean waves are really convincing when it is in 2. This swinging motion seems out of place in *Drink to Me Only*; 6 seems to make it more dignified and expressive.

These examples do not illustrate points 2 above. Suppose a ⁴⁄₄ piece contains many sforzandos or loud entrances on beats 2 and 4;

the conductor can help the performers more by beating in 4, as he can thus make sharp motions on beats 2 and 4; if he is conducting in 2 it is much harder to help. In the last movement of Stravinsky's *Symphonie de psaumes* there is a lengthy section in ²⁄₂ in which chorus and horns have many such entrances. We found that these were hard to sing and play in 2, but immediately improved in 4. Subsequently a revised edition came out indicating that the section in question should be conducted in 4! (See note above about the infallibility of composers.)

As for points 3, if a certain piece tends to drag, use fewer beats; if it frequently runs ahead, use more. The writer has found that both orchestra and chorus tend to slow down in the furious Dies Irae in Mozart's Requiem; although the movement really feels like "4" it has been necessary to do it in 2 to keep it fast. The Lacrymosa, on the other hand, although ideally conducted in a very slow 4, sometimes has tended to creep ahead, especially if the singers could not hear the violins. In those cases it was necessary to conduct in 12.

A conductor must consider these points at great length, and frequently review his thinking about works which he considers familiar. Much of the success or failure of at least half the pieces he conducts may depend on how wisely he decides whether to do more or fewer beats. This point cannot be stressed too strongly.

ASSIGNMENTS

Beginners:
1. Learn the basic principles stated in this chapter and think about them for the rest of your life.
2. For review (not related to this chapter), look at the faults listed under Assignment 4 for professionals in Chapter VII. Are you developing any of these? If so, take emergency action to eliminate them before they become ingrained habits.

Professionals:
1. If all this is familiar to you, reconsider every piece you are working on at present and see whether some might perhaps go better with more or fewer beats.

CHAPTER XVI

MOULDING THE MUSIC

It would be quite possible for someone to perform all the actions described in this volume correctly and yet have a poor technique. Mechanical clarity is not enough. The conductor must constantly remember to "mould the music" with his actions, somewhat as though he were shaping clay. Each motion should portray in visual terms what he feels the music should sound like. If it dances, beat patterns are not enough; his arms, his face, even his head and shoulders must also dance. If it is somber and sustained, all his motions must contribute to this mood. Even minor structural divisions should be shown by some almost indefinable half shrug or breath.

For example, take the Hallelujah Chorus from Handel's *Messiah* (this is chosen as everyone can think it from memory while reading the following). The orchestral introduction should start with a positive downbeat and three subsidiaries; then the music repeats itself almost exactly, and so should the conductor; next there is a bar of only moderate intensity, preceded by an eighth note anacrusis.

In bar 4 the chorus enters. The conductor should make this entrance even more intense than the opening, and much more so than bar 3; bar 5 is the same as bar 4, only there must be a crisp "hot stove" bounce at the end to help the chorus with the sixteenths. The next bar (6) is more dance-like than anything so far; in bar 7, we must sense a certain temporary finality at the cadence on the third beat; beat four should be quite small, but it must bounce high for the next "Hallelujah" entrance, which is like bar 4. The whole structure of bars 8, 9, 10, and 11 is the same as 4 through 7 and should be conducted the same, though possibly more intensely. In bar 12 ("for the Lord God . . .") a broader feeling is probably desirable, with a long line lasting until halfway through bar 14; the beats should bounce less high and have more sideways

movement, to imply a stretching sideways of the line rather than
vertical emphasis. Then there are two more bars of dance-like faster
notes. All this time the conductor must virtually hypnotize the
performers into creating a mood of supreme exultation.

The detail of interpretation above is open to debate, but the concept of constantly changing the style of conducting as required to
mould the music is not.

Anyone who has been fortunate enough to watch Stokowski has
seen a supreme master of "moulding the music." Every nuance,
every subtlety is portrayed in his motions. He can caress a gentle
melody or whip a percussion section into furious action. Yet in a
work unfamiliar to the players he makes every technical point clear.

How is a student to learn this all-important aspect of conducting?

1. By mastering his technique so that it is subservient to his musical wishes.

2. By telling himself to *conduct*—that is, to throw himself into
the task of drawing music from the performers rather than merely
going through studied mechanical actions.

3. By *loving* the music he conducts, and losing himself in it.

ASSIGNMENTS

Beginners and professionals:

1. (This calls for privacy. Lock out your faithful friends this
time.) Put on your currently favorite record and throw yourself
into conducting it, with very little thought about technique.
Then concentrate for a few moments on technique. Then
dance with no inhibitions whatever and no thought of conducting. Bound all over the room. Interpret the music with
your whole body. Then gradually modify your actions so that
they eventually merge into a correct conducting technique, but
still retain the emotional and structural qualities you showed
in your dancing.

Chapter XVII

FERMATAS

The simple matter of a fermata at the end of a composition was discussed in Chapter XIV. The troublesome kind are those followed by more music.

The problem is never the fermata itself. Simply hold the hand still when you come to the fermata, letting the note continue as long as you wish. Like falling out of the Empire State Building, the trouble comes when you stop.

In general there are three types of fermatas. The writer classifies them by what happens after the fermata itself. (The techniques for conducting them are quite general although the classification is original, as far as is known.) They are:

A. Fermatas with no period of silence or "cut" after them. The sound continues uninterrupted.

B. Those followed by a short period of silence (usually about one beat in length).

C. Those followed by a long period of silence (considerably longer than one beat).

Modern composers generally indicate which of these they wish; with older masters the interpreter rarely has any help and must decide for himself. (Wide differences of opinion usually result. The fermatas near the end of Beethoven's Second Symphony, for example, were treated by Toscanini as type A, by Bruno Walter as type B, and by Weingartner as type C. Each was a noted authority on Beethoven. This provides food for thought on the authoritativeness of Noted Authorities.)

Type A Fermatas: No Cut Afterwards

1. Beat the fermata and hold it as long as you wish at the bottom of the beat on the "bounce level."

2. Continue smoothly into the next beat. As your hand was resting at the "bounce level" it will of course have to move upwards before coming down for the next beat.

3. The left hand can help. Hold it out motionless during the fermata, and mirror the right hand when it starts moving again.

Note: The problem in Type A is to prevent the performers from cutting off before the next note.

Fermata on 3 in a 3 pattern:

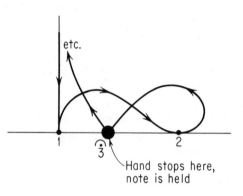

Type B Fermatas: Short Cut Afterwards

1. Beat the fermata and hold it at the bottom of the "bounce level."

2. Repeat the beat on which the fermata occurred and continue. As your hand was resting on the "bounce level" its first motion will be upward for a short distance before hitting downward again. This downward motion (repeating the beat) acts as a cut-off and also is a preliminary for the next note.

The length of the silence is shown by how long you take between the cut-off and the next bounce. This type can be used for various lengths of cuts, from very short to slightly longer than one beat. Most of the time musicians instinctively make it exactly one beat.

3. The left hand may assist, as in Type A.

This is by far the most common form of fermata:

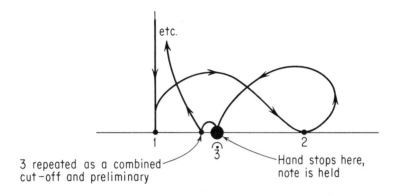

3 repeated as a combined
cut-off and preliminary

Hand stops here,
note is held

Type C Fermatas: Long Cut Afterwards

1. Beat the fermata and hold it at the bottom of the beat on the "bounce level."
2. Give a cut-off as described in Chapter XIV.
3. Hold still as long as desired.
4. Continue as though starting a new piece, with a preliminary, or if the music starts between beats, two preliminaries.

This type is used for a long, dramatic pause:

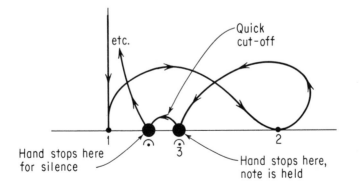

Hand stops here
for silence

Hand stops here,
note is held

Further Points About Fermatas

WARNING

Be sure not to interchange types B and C. If you make a cut-off *and* a preliminary beat during a short period of silence the action is hurried and confused; if you try to make the cut-off act also as the preliminary beat during a long silence, the motion is much too slow.

Note: Some conductors use a slow upward motion for a fermata, on the grounds that this prevents the sound from dying away. With a well-trained group this produces an unwanted crescendo.

DRILL

Useful practice can be gained at this point by applying these techniques to the last four bars of *America* (*God Save the Queen*). (Never mind whether the fermata is artistically justifiable; this is a technical drill.)

From ev - 'ry moun - tain side   let   free - dom   ring!
Long   to   reign o - ver us;   God save the   Queen.

CHANGING TEMPOS

Frequently the music after a fermata is in a new tempo, such as an allegro following the slow introduction of a symphony. The techniques described above should be exactly the same, with the preliminary beat (which is also the cut-off beat in type B fermatas) indicating the new tempo.

FERMATAS ON LONG NOTES

Frequently the fermata is placed on a long note. The conductor should give all the necessary beats and actually put the fermata on the final beat of the note, or else orchestral players may mix up their counting.

Thus in this case:

$$\frac{4}{4} \overset{\frown}{} \, \text{♩} \, |$$

the conductor beats 1, 2, and 3, pausing on 3.
In this case:

$$\frac{2}{4} \text{♩} \_\_ | \overset{\frown}{} \, |$$

he must beat the complete first bar and give both beats in the second, pausing on 2.

(In such cases the beats after the long note commences should be quite small.)

FERMATAS BETWEEN BEATS

In cases like the following:

Allegro (in 2)

$$\frac{6}{8} \text{♫♪ ♫♪} | \text{♪}\overset{\frown}{\text{♪}} \, \text{♫♪} |$$

give "1" of the second bar and hold still while the music continues to the fermata. Then proceed normally.

COMPLEX FERMATAS

Every so often one comes across a situation not covered adequately by the techniques above. Long lists and abstruse instructions are of little help. It is felt that the reader will do best to solve such problems as they arise, in the following manner (after he has made sure that the above techniques cannot be applied).

1. Use your common sense to figure out something else.
2. Try it in rehearsal a few times.
3. If it doesn't work try something different.

This procedure will solve many complex problems. (See Preface for advice on bridge crossing.)

ASSIGNMENTS

Beginners:

1. Get together again with the blackboard, the chalk, and your two faithful friends. Write a number of possibilities on the board and see if you can make your friends sing them (monotone), without telling them in advance which type of fermata to expect. A few possibilities are listed below; make up others yourself.

Professionals:

1. You are probably thoroughly experienced in conducting fermatas. Be critical of your cut-offs, however. Many fairly successful conductors are ambiguous on cut-offs, with either too little preliminary indication, or a violent motion that breaks the mood and looks like another downbeat.

2. Write a few exercises in unusual time signatures and test yourself. For example:

CHAPTER XVIII

EARS

It has been said that a good conductor is merely a pair of ears with arms attached. While this statement may slight the intellectual requirements of the art, it contains a great deal of truth.

As the physical actions of conducting become more and more automatic the student must increase the amount of his attention devoted to listening. When we conductors hear our own tapes we sometimes are dismayed at the errors that escaped us. It seems as though our ears must retract into our heads the minute we lift up our arms.

Professional conductors reading the above may be encouraged to find that others also have this depressing experience. It is easily explained. When we conduct we are attending to many duties, and when we listen we have no other responsibilities or distractions. Nevertheless, we must do everything in our power to increase the amount we hear while conducting. Suggestions:

1. Improve your arm technique so that it almost takes care of itself, like working a car's controls in traffic. If you have practised conducting a piece sufficiently you can concentrate more on listening to it.

2. You must constantly remind yourself to listen. A well-known corporation hangs a sign saying THINK in all its offices. Our slogan must be LISTEN.

3. Be sure that your hearing is physiologically in good shape. Wax in ears can only be detected by a doctor and may filter out certain overtones. A music lover whose hearing seemed normal was found during a routine medical check-up to have wax in his ears. When this was removed the whole world sounded different. He attended a recital by a fine string quartet and could hardly stand the tone. He was so unaccustomed to high frequencies that he found normal brilliance unbearably brittle. Think what his group might have sounded like had he been a conductor! Long, thick hair worn

over the ears has been shown to have a similar effect temporarily—
women conductors please note!

4. You must develop your ear as much as possible. Natural hearing ability is relatively unimportant, although of course there are
individual differences. (This is fortunate, or we all would reach our
professional peak in our early 'teens and then decline.) Traditional
ear training courses are of little help. When in their careers are
conductors ever required to take down four-part harmony played
on a piano, other than to pass courses? The most useful type of
training is in wrong note detection, where the instructor plays or
conducts passages containing deliberate wrong notes and the class
members try to locate them while following their scores.

Even this is not much help, as there are not enough class hours
available for such a subject. The conductor must train himself.
Listening to a concert or records and following all parts, separately
and together, is useful. Attending someone else's rehearsal and following a score is better—trying to find errors before the conductor.

The student must of course also learn the timbres of different
instruments and voices, and must develop his aural imagination.
Conducting in silence will help, as suggested in Chapter XIII.

Erich Leinsdorf once suggested to the writer when he was a student that he form and conduct a string quartet, primarily for practice in detecting wrong notes. Coaching any small ensemble would
be equally beneficial.

ASSIGNMENTS

Beginners:
    1. Make every effort to get experience in detecting wrong notes.
       Ask your friend to play simple pieces, like hymns, with occa-
       sional deliberate errors—some conspicuous, some subtle.
    2. Take on pupils; coach any small vocal or instrumental group.
Professionals:
    1. Hang a large LISTEN sign where you can see it during all your
       rehearsals!
    2. Have your ears examined occasionally.

CHAPTER XIX

NERVES

Excellent training and superb talent are useless if the performer is too nervous to use them in public. The composer, the coach, and the teacher may do their work in private, but the concert artist must sooner or later walk out and face that sea of faces. To the person who has taken part in few concerts, or the experienced musician who still becomes nervous, here are a few ideas which have helped many a young musician.

1. You must be thoroughly prepared. Start work early so that you are completely secure in the music.

2. You should not plan to extend your technique to the utmost in public; you may not quite make it. Keep something in reserve in case you are below par. Do not play your hardest piece, your fastest tempo, or your highest note. A composition you occasionally manage to struggle through in a studio is not suitable for the pressures of a concert.

In conducting, be sure you can do a Brahms symphony in private before you tackle Mozart in public; conquer the complexities of Stravinsky or Britten in your own room before risking Brahms at a concert. You need a *reserve of technique.*

3. Remember that you are not the first person to be scared stiff before an event. Most people are, including some of the finest athletes. Knowing that you are in good company may cheer you up.

4. Try not to let the concert alter your normal routine unduly. Have adequate rest, but carry on with most of your regular tasks. Taking two days off beforehand and sitting at home alone brooding about it may give you a bad case of the jitters.

5. Ask yourself what you really fear. Suppose it *is* a fiasco, and you run off the stage with the audience throwing vegetables. You could try again, or start a new life. Schumann developed as a composer only after he hurt his finger and abandoned a concert career.

93

(Naturally, it is to be hoped such a thing won't happen—but thinking it through to the end seems to reduce the fear.)

6. Try to see life in proper perspective. Is a bad concert really a terrible tragedy?

7. Don't worry about minor errors. Performances are never perfect. A recently issued recording of a celebrated pianist contains more than 100 splices to remove errors. The audience rarely notices little mistakes and understands that they are bound to occur.

8. Say to yourself, "Well, I guess you really aren't up to this concert. Too bad. You'd better phone so-and-so and ask him to take your place on the program . . . I'm sure he'd love to have the chance." This is almost foolproof.

9. Act to one and all as though you are not nervous. The more you tell everybody what a wreck you are the worse you'll become. The steadier you pretend to be the sooner you will calm yourself down.

10. When you walk out on the stage, you may still feel somewhat wobbly. That is natural. Don't worry about it. But then you must FORGET THE AUDIENCE AND ENJOY MAKING MUSIC! Music is for enjoyment. If you worry about the audience during the performance your tension will increase. On the other hand, by concentrating exclusively on the music your nervousness will soon subside. If you make a mistake, put it instantly out of your mind. Enjoy yourself and so will the audience.

ASSIGNMENTS

Beginners:

    1. Find a nervous recitalist and quote from memory the points above. It will be good practice for working on yourself when your turn comes.

Professionals:

    1. Everyone expects you to be the tower of strength. These suggestions may help you keep yourself steady. Radiate confidence even when there is no reason whatsoever for having any. And remember, the success of the concert may depend on the extent to which you have calmed down your performers, especially young soloists.

CHAPTER XX

THOUGHTS ON INTERPRETATION

Interpretation requires a lifetime of study, and many excellent books are appearing on the subject. This chapter will merely present some general ideas and suggestions.

There are two opposing ideals in musical performance. On the one hand, we can be purely subjective and personal in our interpretation of the printed page. On the other, we can conscientiously try to re-create the musical ideas of the composer, aided by his markings on the composition itself and similar works, his expressed views on performance, and our knowledge of the conditions and customs of his day.

We can say, "I am the co-artist. The composer is not responsible for this concert. I know as much about music as he does and more about my own group and hall. I shall play this piece any way I want. My audience is accustomed to modern sound. I feel free to change anything the composer indicated, including the notes themselves." Or we can say, "I am merely the builder who follows the composer's blueprints in re-creating this masterpiece."

The first approach seems egotistical to most musicians today, but was recently widespread. There are still musicians who modernize even Bach to suit themselves. The writer once heard a world-famous actor say "the important thing isn't SHAKESPEARE's Hamlet, it's OLIVIER's Hamlet, or GIELGUD's Hamlet, or MY Hamlet. Thus each performance is new and vital." This statement seemed shocking at the time, but on reconsideration must be conceded to be a valid viewpoint.

This modernized-subjective approach is, however, usually the result of ignorance, poor taste, or lack of musical insight rather than a positive philosophy. Pianists follow a certain Italian editor's fussy romanticisms in Bach because they have never experienced the awesome grandeur of a great baroque performance. A celebrated English conductor adds copious brass throughout Handel's *Israel in Egypt.* This is not only anachronistic and unfair to the composer's ideas; it becomes tedious and ineffective. For example, in the final chorus (the rousing "horse and the riders"), Handel carefully leaves off his trumpets until about two-thirds of the way through. When they finally come in the result is nothing short of hair-raising. In the recording mentioned above this effect is totally lost because of the Berliozian clatter which precedes it.

The second, or historical-objective approach, is the ideal to which most sincere performers attain today. Musical scholarship is at a high level, and ancient instruments are now readily available which thirty years ago existed only in museums. Most musicians no longer accept Bach on a concert grand piano with nineteenth-century pedal effects but insist on a harpsichord or clavichord. Recorders, harpsichords, and baroque organs are now as common as string quartets.

Scholarship has been of great benefit in revealing the hidden beauties of older music. Playing certain eighteenth-century grace notes in a historically correct manner adds a discordant pungency which spices the otherwise bland harmony. Improvising variations in the *da capo* section of an aria is not only authentic but spares us from tedious literal repetitions never intended by the composer. Innumerable other illustrations could be given to show that historical accuracy also improves artistic quality. In Winton Dean's book, *Handel's Dramatic Oratorios and Masques,** he convincingly states the case for historically correct performances: ". . . many modern performances of the oratorios are travesties. . . . There is an enormous amount of spring-cleaning to be done before the filth of ages is stripped from Handel's music. . . .

"This is not a matter of pedantry; we need not plead piety towards Handel's memory; aesthetic pleasure alone provides sufficient motive. Handel was a far greater composer . . . than the English public is allowed to know. . . . False traditions of performance [have] reduced the music to a synthetic suet that revolts the stomachs of sensitive listeners. It has lost its freshness, depth, and proportion, like a picture coated with layers of discoloured varnish. . . .

"There is no ground for supposing that a modern audience, how-

* Oxford University Press, 1959, pp. 102, 114.

ever untutored, appreciates Handel only when he is brought up to date. Indeed the evidence is the other way: when the dirt is removed, the public is often quicker than the professional musician, for whom the varnish is as sacred as the old master, to appreciate the variety and colour that lie beneath."

He continues in an interesting footnote, "There is a parallel in the cleaned pictures at the National Gallery, which delighted the public but caused a bitter controversy among painters."

The historical approach has been discredited sometimes by the sad fact that the fine musicologist is not always a great artist. Some early recordings of historically accurate performances were often dismally unmusical.

Another weakness in the historical movement has been the old fault of a little knowledge being a dangerous thing. Ardent historians sometimes seize on one fact and ignore others. Bach once wrote a letter saying that he needed at least sixteen singers to perform major works for double chorus. A New York conductor therefore gave a performance of the St. Matthew Passion in Carnegie Hall using exactly sixteen choristers. In his sincere effort to honor Bach's intentions he ignored the following:

1. Bach wanted *at least* sixteen singers and might have been thrilled to death to have had more.

2. Modern string players probably produce a larger tone than was possible in Bach's day (due to the difference in bow and neck), thereby destroying Bach's balance.

3. Bach's churches were smaller and much more resonant than Carnegie Hall, with more stone surfaces and less carpet and drapery.

4. Carnegie Hall in winter is very hot, the top gallery usually in the high 80's. The St. Matthew Passion was premiered in April. As every North American knows who has ever shivered through a European winter, even today a church would rarely be above 55° F. (The standard temperature for mercury barometers is 50°, this figure having been chosen by European meteorologists on the grounds that that is the average temperature *indoors* in Europe throughout the year!) This alone would mean that Bach's churches probably were much more resonant than Carnegie Hall. Even a difference of a few degrees alters the acoustics of a hall to the point where it may

ruin the tone of a group. For these reasons Bach's congregation doubtess felt far more emotional impact in the loud passages than did the poor frustrated souls in Carnegie Hall.

This illustrates some of the difficulties and dangers of the historical approach. Numerous other barriers prevent our hearing music exactly as the older composers did.

We must also ask ourselves whether the Masters were really happy with their performing conditions. Conductors usually reduce the size of an orchestra when playing Mozart. A little-known statement by the composer himself provides considerable evidence to doubt the wisdom of such a practice. In a letter to his father from Vienna written on April 11, 1781, he describes a recent performance of one of his symphonies, possibly K.338 in C major: "I forgot to tell you the other day that at the concert the symphony went *magnifique* and had the greatest success. There were forty violins, the wind-instruments were all doubled, there were ten violas, ten double basses, eight violoncellos and six bassoons."* Perhaps conductors should *augment* their orchestras if they want to play Mozart symphonies as the composer really would have liked!

First performances prepared under the direction of the composer were not only frequently far from ideal; some of them must have been living nightmares. One such concert took place in the winter of 1808 (and, incidently, marked Beethoven's last public appearance as a pianist). The gargantuan all-Beethoven program included the world premieres of his Fifth and Sixth Symphonies, four movements from his Mass in C, his aria, "Ah, Perfido," the G major Piano Concerto, and the Choral Fantasy, the words for which had just been written. The performers never had a complete rehearsal, and the soprano soloist, after a fight with the composer, refused to sing, and was replaced by a terrified and incompetent understudy. The audience was sparse, the hall in Vienna bitterly cold, and the program lasted four hours. Beethoven caused chaos by playing a repeat that had been canceled, the clarinets came in early, and the pianist-composer stood up and hurled several sentences of invective at them before making them play it over.

---

* Letter 398, page 1076, Vol. III, *The Letters of Mozart and His Family,* trans. and ed. by Emily Anderson. Macmillan, 1938.

The frozen audience was apathetic. In the long and terrible history of bizarre concerts, this was surely one of the most bizarre.

Another point against the historical approach is that *composers make mistakes.* Bach's E flat Magnificat is full of errors which he corrected in the D major version of the same work, written a few years later. If he had died before the revision was completed we might still be playing all those wrong notes and even drowning out the trebles with the trumpet in the Suscepit Israel, a balance error remedied in the later version.

Vibrato is even a matter of controversy and confusion. Today it is used by all orchestral players except horns and clarinets, and Reginald Kell is introducing it to the latter instrument. The writer can remember the excitement in Toronto in the 1930's when a bassoonist imported from Detroit played with vibrato. Today it is expected everywhere. In older books a "flute-like tone" meant "steady, without vibrato." Mozart describes in sneering terms a singer whose voice wavered like a tremulant on an organ. English choirboys sing a straight tone but their counterparts in the United States mostly favor vibrato. To use a harpsichord, F trumpet, and recorder in Bach's Second Brandenburg Concerto and then have the solo oboe play with vibrato is considered in some quarters to be as anachronistic as to make a supercolossal motion picture of the landing of William the Conqueror with lavish authentic costumes and aircraft vapor trails across the sky.

An anecdote about Sibelius related by Harold Rogers in *The Christian Science Monitor* shows that at least one great composer could enjoy his music at more than one tempo. The violinist Paul Cherkassky was rehearsing Sibelius's Violin Concerto with the composer. When they came to the second movement, Cherkassky said:

"Maestro, some musicians prefer to take this Adagio at a faster tempo, like this"—demonstrating—"and others prefer it slower, this way"—again demonstrating. "How do you like it?"

Sibelius made the reply, "Both ways."

What, then, are we to do? Try to be authentic, or forget about the composer altogether? Purely subjective performances are questionable; purely historical are virtually impossible. Each musician must select for himself a position somewhere between the two extremes. Although adhering to general principles, he will probably find it necessary to move somewhat one way or the other as he performs different works.

Because of the conflict of ideals in interpretation, we must not give a simple "yes" or "no" when a student asks, "Is it correct to slow down here?" We must reply somewhat as follows: "The composer didn't indicate it. Most authorities think that such retards were not done at that time. I don't feel it's artistic to do so, as it loses the energetic drive you have built up. But I cannot say whether it is *correct* or not."

EDITIONS

One of the barriers to any kind of intelligent or artistic performance is the frequently low caliber of editions readily available. Fortunately this situation is rapidly changing, but newer and more scholarly publications are little known and are usually expensive. Few students realize how many of the interpretation indications on their music are the personal opinions of some publisher's hack. In many cases these represent late 19th-century styles of performance which are rapidly becoming unacceptable. Even the original *Bachgesellschaft* and particularly the *Händelgesellschaft* editions are not as free from sin as one might think.

Some editors with a greater sense of humility try to indicate which are their markings and which those of the composer. Frequently they use smaller type for their own. However, with even the most eminent it is often difficult to tell which type is which when the two sizes are not close together for comparison. Some leading German editions of works by Bach and Brahms are at fault in this respect.

Whether the performer follows the editor's markings or not he should be thoroughly aware of which are the editor's and which the composer's. In many cases he will become convinced that the composer knew more about his own music than the editor.

Students ask how to tell a conscientious, scholarly edition from a spurious one. This is difficult. Be skeptical of any heavily marked piece written before 1800. Performance indications were sparse before that date. Even in later works copiously marked by the composers, some editors find it impossible to keep their sticky little fingers off. Read the small print in the front of the score, and compare your copy whenever possible with one which claims to be an authentic original edition, or "Urtext."

RECORD WORSHIP

Often when a student is asked why he interprets a passage in a certain way, he replies, "Because it's like that on the record." Further questioning frequently reveals that he cannot even remember the name of the performer. He simply assumes that because it is on a record it is divinely inspired and should not be questioned by a mere mortal.

One of the great advantages of studying music in this era is the abundance of low cost records. A comparison of various recordings of the same piece by eminent artists often reveals amazing differences, especially in older music. The case of the fermatas in the Beethoven Second Symphony was mentioned in Chapter XVII; countless other cases could be listed. These show that the student, while treating a recording with respect, should nevertheless use his own knowledge and artistry to arrive at his own interpretation, rather than blindly worshipping any one record. Better still, he should compare in detail every available recording of a work before making final decisions on its performance.

ASSIGNMENT

Beginners and Professionals:

1. To help orient yourself in this vague, personal, complex, and contradictory matter of interpretation, the following chart may be of assistance. See where your current thinking about a few composers is located.

   You may have difficulty placing yourself in general terms, as your approach probably varies with specific elements of performance. Many conductors modernize Beethoven's brass parts but would never omit a movement. Others play the opening bars of *Messiah* as though double dotted, in the style of a French overture, but would faint if the tenor sang Handel's own cadenza at the end of "Every valley"!*

* Published in the Coopersmith edition, Carl Fischer.

PERFORMANCE CHART

HISTORICAL-
OBJECTIVE
EXTREME

MODERNIZED-
SUBJECTIVE
EXTREME

Re-create conditions of first performance as accurately as possible.

Re-create a performance the composer probably would have considered ideal in his own day.

Follow composer's intentions where practical—harpsichord if available, but modern bow, vibrato, etc.

Give the type of performance you feel the composer would have wanted if he had had your group and your hall.

Give the type of performance you feel the composer would want if he were alive today.

Use your musicological knowledge to decide what the composer probably wanted, and select or reject his ideas at will in building your own performance.

Use the printed notes as a source of material for your own creative ability, using full modern performance resources.

CHAPTER XXI

SOME REHEARSAL SUGGESTIONS

Rehearsal techniques are best learned by listening to or participating in rehearsals. See if a specific device used by the conductor actually works. If it does, try it yourself; if not, find a better way.

Techniques should be varied as the need demands. What works with one orchestra, band, or choir may not with another. Interest span, musical background, seriousness of purpose vary from group to group and rehearsal to rehearsal, and techniques must vary also. While conducting technique is more or less universal, rehearsal techniques are personal and specialized.

A conductor should constantly try to think up new approaches. No one is so successful that he cannot improve. The introduction of a new device may add interest and variety to a rehearsal even if it results in comparatively little improvement. On the other hand, too many "gimmicks" will irritate everyone. Most rehearsal time should be spent in improving performance through hard work in the time-honored manner.

As the title of this chapter indicates, no attempt will be made to cover all the knowledge needed to train and rehearse every possible type of musical organization at all levels of ability. This would obviously require a full-size encyclopedia. Instead, it includes a few opinions and suggestions which have proved successful, some of which are not widely known. Many important subjects are not even mentioned, there being an abundance of good books in this field.

EMOTION

The ability to feel the emotion in a musical passage depends partly on musical background, but mostly on whether or not the conductor can show the performers what the emotion should be. In rehearsals, this may be done by:

1. Conducting technique, including facial expression, etc.

103

2. Use of musical terms (maestoso, cantabile, etc.)

3. Short English phrases ("gracefully," "with fire," etc.)

4. A description of the dramatic situation as the composer sees it. (This is of course only possible in program music or music with words.)

5. An analogy not connected with the music, but evoking a similar mood. ("Sing as though you have just received some wonderful news.")

6. Sometimes exaggerated gestures are helpful—a sweeping motion that would be unacceptable in concert, or a foot stamp. These should not be resorted to frequently or the concert will seem tame to the performers by comparison.

Many a conductor spoils a concert by over-conducting at rehearsals. To prevent this, the best method with an experienced group is usually to make sure that the last few rehearsals are on a low emotional level, deliberately under-conducting, with frequent stops and starts. The concert usually "takes off" after this type of preparation, but few people have the nerve to risk it. They make their final rehearsals just like the concert, which as a result may sound a trifle stale.

TONE AND INTONATION

These would require a separate book. They are listed here to emphasize their importance.

DYNAMICS

Even volume. With most untrained singers, the problem is to make them sing loudly without harshness. This is a matter of tone plus emotion. The same is true of instruments.

A true pp is hard to achieve on a solo instrument or voice, but is a simple matter with a large group. Each individual must play much more quietly than possible in a solo. If the tone actually stops for a second altogether it does not matter, if others are on the same note. Tell them, "if you hear yourself you're too loud," and it works wonders. This leaves one or two who have to be reminded personally, by look, gesture, or rifle.

Do not waste the intensity of good pianissimos by drilling notes at this volume level. Let them come up to "p" or "mf" for drill, and the pianissimos will be satisfactory in run-throughs.

Sudden changes. These require constant work, plus good conducting. If necessary, take the loud place several times, pause, then do the quiet one. Decrease the number of times and the length of the pause until the change is as desired.

Cresc. and dim. These dynamic effects developed last in music, and are the hardest to perform. If necessary, take the highest point, then the lowest point, and then move from one to the other in slow time. Each performer must gauge his own volume. The long orchestral crescendos in Rossini overtures often need this drill.

RHYTHM

Assuming that the performers understand the arithmetic, rhythmical problems can usually be solved by insisting that everyone think the smallest convenient time value. This also helps prevent running ahead. For example, in a passage in slow pizzicato quarter notes, the normal tendency to run can be helped if the players think continuous sixteenths.

This should also help the numerous simple rhythms which are often slightly inaccurate and which lead to sloppy performance or even actual breakdown, such as

Slowing down. This usually results from insecurity of notes, trouble with words, or fingering or bowing problems. Locate and cure the cause and the dragging ceases. (Or as stated in Chapter IX, use smaller beats, or fewer beats in a bar, as discussed in Chapter XV.)

Late entrances. These may be caused by timidity, lack of knowledge of the music, or failing to think the speed of the little notes before the entrances. *The performer must not rest during a rest!* He must work harder than when he is playing.

In vocal music, singers must remember to sing preliminary consonants as though they were grace notes before the beat, because the vowel sets the tempo. The second movement of most masses starts late because the singers start the word "gloria" on the beat, instead of saying the "g" and the "l" before and the "o" on the beat. Have them sing "oria" a few times and then put the "gl" in early, like nineteenth-century grace notes.

Singers and wind players will also lose time if they try to breathe in a short rest. They must either breathe faster, take in less air, or stagger the breathing (that is, everyone breathes at different times). This is essential if there are several consonants before and after a rest—try saying "hosts have" in a hurry, with a breath in the middle!

Never let down the good performers. If they come in ahead of the others, correct the laggards to bring them up to the best. The good ones must not feel conspicuous and wrong, or soon they'll stop coming in on time and then nobody will.

ACCENTS

Often accents are carefully observed by performers but the effect is lost because they put on another accent nearby. This is particularly prevalent when the accent is immediately before the bar line; the player will add another on the downbeat, obscuring the first. Try making them count out loud . . . "one . . . two . . . three . . . FOUR . . . one . . . two . . .", etc. Until they can *think* the accent in the proper place *and avoid accents elsewhere* they cannot sing or play it.

When there is a fp or sf at the start of a long note, many people play the whole note loud—this is simply f, not sf. Be sure they reduce the volume to its normal level after the accented beginning.

PHRASING

This is largely a matter of having the parts marked properly and describing the effect desired. Tonguing, bowing, and choice of breathing places are involved. It is an interpretative problem rather than a direct concern of rehearsal techniques.

FOLLOWING THE CONDUCTOR

The finest conducting technique is useless if nobody sees it. Many performers feel they are watching when they see a blurry motion out of the corner of their eye. Others think it is necessary to look up only at tempo changes. None of these musicians ever has a true rapport with the conductor, and through him the other players.

The best way to find out whether these people are really watching is to change tempo drastically at some point where it is neither expected nor musical. The inattentive musicians are soon playing a canon with the others. It is sometimes the only way to convince them that they cannot see through their eyelids.

On the other hand, some conductors stop unexpectedly to see who is watching. Even the best player looks at the music for two or three seconds at a time and may come blasting out by himself and feel foolish. He soon loses his confident style of playing. The first method shows faults without unduly embarrassing the poor fellow, as there is still sound continuing.

The group should be trained to watch from the first rehearsal, or sensitivity will not be developed. When sight-reading they must have the point hammered home that "the time you need to watch the conductor the most is the FIRST time, because you know the music the least." Of course, a few minor mistakes will result, but these are unimportant compared with the greater error of letting them play with their eyes continually down.

GIVING THE PLACE

One minor matter should be mentioned which frequently loses time and causes irritation at rehearsals. When some conductors give the place in the score they locate it in the order in which it occurs to *them*. They say, "There should be an accent on the F sharp on the fourth beat of the fifth bar after letter B in the second violin part." The players cannot start hunting until the sentence is finished, by which time they have forgotten the beginning. Count out loud so the players can keep up with you, and word the instructions in the order *they* need to find the place: for example, "Second violins; after letter B, bar one, two, three, four, five; fourth beat, there should be an accent on the F sharp." By the time you finish the sentence they will have found the note.

This is like addressing an envelope; we write from top to bottom, but the postal authorities obviously must read the address from bottom to top.

GENERAL

Unlike a bride, a rehearsal does not require something borrowed and something blue, but it does need something old and something new. Most rehearsals should have variety of musical activity, and therefore should contain the following:

1. something not seen before
2. drill, with stops and repetition (or no improvement will result)
3. straight run-throughs.

Obviously, as the concert approaches, there can be little or no new music, and in early rehearsals a weak group may not be able to do straight runs.

If all the music is introduced and read at the beginning of the season, the interest advantage of investigating "something new" is lost.

Rehearsals also need variety of emotion. Avoid staying too long in any one musical mood, if at all possible. Change the general tone of the rehearsal as the situation demands. At times the conductor may be casual, imploring, flippant, angry, intense, patient, humorous, or excited. Nothing leads to a devitalized performance as fast as a conductor who is invariably calm and suave.

Good performance is not only a matter of training and knowledge, but also of being warmed up and in the right frame of mind. A cold, tired, and bored group can sound horrible. Under such conditions it is a waste of time to try to improve separate details, such as intonation, rhythm, dynamics, etc., or to strive for finesse in isolated passages. Change the mood and everything will suddenly improve, even including sight-reading ability.

If the trouble has not cleared up after some straightforward playing or singing, try a different piece, take a slow passage at breakneck speed, make them stand up and stretch, tell a joke, have them give each other a back rub, read the riot act, or have a coffee break—in short, try anything. If all fails, it may be advisable to dismiss the rehearsal and hope they will be back to normal when you next meet. (See also page 122 for pre-concert warm-ups.)

ASSIGNMENTS

Beginners:

1. Join every performing group you possibly can.
2. Spend much time visiting other rehearsals. No matter how good or bad the group or the conductor, you can always learn (even if what *not* to do).

Professionals:

1. Try to find time to perform under someone else.
2. Same as point 2 for beginners.

CHAPTER XXII

SOLOS AND RECITATIVES

Solos

The relation between soloist and conductor is at best a total union of souls and at worst a cold war. Before the first rehearsal they must work on the music together and agree on interpretation. Also, at all doubtful points it should be clearly decided who leads and who follows.

With musicians of equal status it is customary for the soloist's wishes to prevail. Wherever possible he plays according to his own wishes and the orchestra or chorus follows, accompanying as would a pianist. There are certain passages, however, where the conductor must lead; for example, an opening chord, tutti with soloist. The players cannot see the soloist well enough to come in together. In such places the soloist follows the conductor as though he were an orchestra member. Likewise, cut-offs on fermatas and certain sudden tempo changes are best handled if the conductor temporarily assumes the lead. Afterwards it reverts to the soloist.

If the soloist is considerably junior to the conductor, as when a chorus member sings a short passage alone, he may prefer to follow the conductor. Where several soloists sing a difficult ensemble together with chorus and orchestra, it is preferable for each to look upon himself as another instrument and be completely subservient to the conductor. This homogenizes the style and improves the balance and precision, but it sometimes deflates the ego of the singer. Beethoven's *Missa Solemnis* benefits from both results.

When there is an important solo in a symphonic work the conductor may ask the first desk man to lead as though it were a concerto. (For example, the horn melody at the start of the slow movement in Tchaikovsky's Fifth Symphony.) This usually gratifies the player and results in a better and more soloistic performance.

TECHNIQUE

The best method of following a soloist is to anticipate rather than wait until the last minute; sing or play the solo with him mentally. As far as technique is concerned, remember the following:

1. If he moves ahead sooner than you anticipated, move the beat gradually faster to catch up. Do not make sudden lightning-fast motions or nobody will see them.

2. If he slows down, such as at an *espressivo*, take your time on the way up, not the way down. Lift your arm higher and move down at the usual rate, rather than "put the brakes" on a beat just before it reaches the bottom. Otherwise everyone is fooled and comes in early.

Recitatives

The interpretation of recitatives is outside the scope of this book. They are probably harder to conduct than any other type of music. Soloist and conductor must work in advance as much as possible, but they still cannot memorize every tempo change exactly, as the performance may vary each time.

TECHNIQUE

Give all the beats, but when the accompaniment is held through two or more counts, make the later beats small, and use a large beat preceded by a clear anticipatory motion each time the accompaniment has a new chord. For example:

This is the way   to con-duct re - ci-ta-tive

Give a clear up and downbeat to start, as in any piece; then make very small beats for 2, 3, 4, and 1 of the next bar. They need not coincide with the soloist (some conductors even give them as fast as possible and then wait for the singer). As he starts the second bar be very alert; bounce high after 2 so as to warn the orchestra that the next chord is coming, and give a clear and large 3 as the singer starts "-tive." These diagrams may help to illustrate the above:

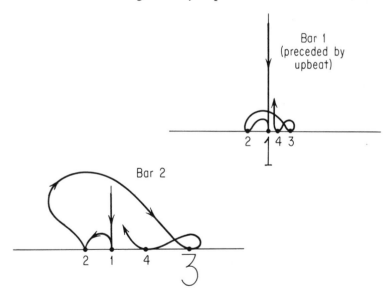

If the accompaniment is played on keyboard alone a conductor probably does more harm than good and should stay out of it; with

the more historically correct method of using one or more lower instruments as well as keyboard most people find it easier with a conductor, *if he can conduct recitatives!*

OPERATIC RECITATIVES

In opera the singer frequently has several bars of recitative without any accompaniment. The tempo may be very free, governed
by considerable stage action. In such cases it is traditional to give
only the first beat of each bar. Some conductors give all downbeats
in quick succession and then wait until the end of the passage before raising their arms to recommence. This is rather hard on the
player who wants to "service" his instrument, as he has no idea
how much time is available. By giving each downbeat as it occurs
the conductor helps the player to judge how much time is left to
drain a horn, change reeds, fix a slipping peg, etc.

ASSIGNMENTS
Beginners:
1. Conduct to records frequently. In addition to other benefits,
   this provides good training for following soloists.
2. Accompany soloists as much as possible on the piano, to develop your own flexibility and sensitivity.
3. Follow recordings and broadcasts of concertos and arias whenever possible.
4. Leave recitatives alone for the present.
Professionals:
1. Practise conducting at sight recitatives in recordings of
   Handel's oratorios and Mozart's operas.

Chapter XXIII

CHANGING BEAT UNITS

Up to this point all rhythmical difficulties have been handled by either preserving the beat pattern, as with syncopations, or changing it, as when a time signature changes from $\frac{4}{4}$ to $\frac{3}{4}$. This takes care of most of the world's music.

However, since Stravinsky's *Le Sacre du printemps* (1913), a number of pieces have been written in which the entire unit of beat must be changed, as when going from $\frac{4}{4}$ to $\frac{3}{8}$.

Consider the following illustration:

The tempo is so fast that in the $\frac{4}{4}$ bars it is only possible to beat quarter notes; eighths would be confused and flustered. On the other hand, quarter notes cannot be beaten in the $\frac{3}{8}$ bar as they would come out uneven, with half a beat left over at the start of the next bar. (This should not be confused with a simple triplet, where the three eighths occupy the space of one quarter note. The eighths here are of the same length as those in the $\frac{4}{4}$ bars but are grouped in threes.)

One school of thought recommends elongating the beat to equal a dotted quarter; thus one beat is given in the $\frac{3}{8}$ bar.

The preferred method was taught at Tanglewood under Stanley Chapple. He had discussed the problem at great length with Koussevitzky, Bernstein, Copland (in whose music such rhythms abound), and members of the Boston Symphony Orchestra. The consensus was that it is clearer to beat the $\frac{3}{8}$ in three. These three fast beats seem easier to follow than one slow floating motion. The writer has observed Stravinsky using the same technique in conducting his own music. The rule may be stated as follows: WHEN THE BEAT UNIT MUST CHANGE, USE FASTER BEATS.

(One important qualification must be made: Keep the fast beats small. At high speeds they should be little more than flicks of the wrist. A large, unwieldy motion slows the tempo.)

If a series of fast ⅜ bars conducted one in a bar is followed by duple quarters, such as ²⁄₄, change to 2 in a bar in the ²⁄₄, beating quarters, rather than one slow beat equal to a half note. The rule still applies—faster beats are used, in this case moving from a dotted quarter to a quarter. For example:

When a change from quarters to a faster unit, such as eighths, must be maintained for several bars, continuous fast threes may be too fussy and it may be preferable to beat dotted quarters. For example:

In all these cases much depends on the context, tempo, character of the piece, and the group. A conductor should follow the rules given above but should keep an eye open for passages where the other method may be more successful (i.e. changing to longer notes).

The same principle should be followed in such a passage as:

It is too fast to beat eighth notes throughout. It will be seen that the ⅝ is really either a ²⁄₄ with one eighth note added at the end, or a ¾ with one eighth removed from the end. Rather than beat a quarter and a dotted quarter, follow the rule and use faster beats: that is, use a 3 pattern, allowing two eighths on the downbeat, two more on the 2 beat, and then a fast 3rd beat for the final eighth, making sure to keep it small. Thus the hand will trace more or less the pattern of a standard three with a small 3rd beat, but the time elapsed between 3 and 1 of the next bar will be equal to one eighth instead of a quarter:

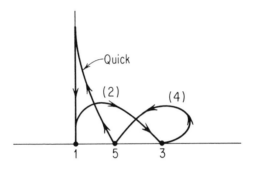

The 7 likewise could be considered a ¾ with an extra eighth note on the end or a ⁴⁄₄ with one missing; use a 4 pattern, beating three quarters, and on the last beat move twice as fast going into the *next downbeat*:

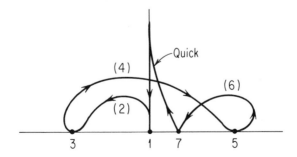

Similarly, the following should be observed:

Allegro

$\frac{5}{8}$ ♩♪ ♪♪♩ | ♪♪♩ ♪♩ |$\frac{7}{8}$ ♩♪ ♩♪ ♪♪♩ | ♪♪♩ ♩♪ ♪♩ |

Beat ♩ ♩ ♪ ♩ ♪ ♩   ♩ ♩ ♩ ♪ ♩ ♪ ♩ ♩

The first and third bars have been discussed above. In the second, this is either a ²⁄₄ with the front half elongated or a ³⁄₄ with the second beat shortened. For conducting purposes consider it the latter.

The fourth bar could be a ³⁄₄ with the first beat stretched or a ⁴⁄₄ with the 2nd shortened. Make it the latter.

Thus the whole passage would be:

Bar 1: a three with the last beat short, as before:

♩ ♩ ♪

Bar 2: a three with the second beat short:

♩ ♪♩

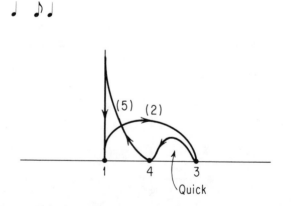

Bar 3: a four with the last beat short, as before:

♩ ♩ ♩ ♪

Bar 4: a four with the second beat short:

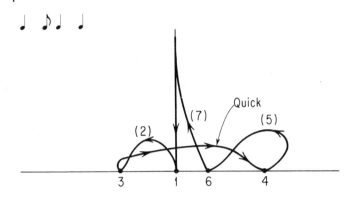

Other unequal divisions of complex time signatures can be dealt
with similarly; for example:

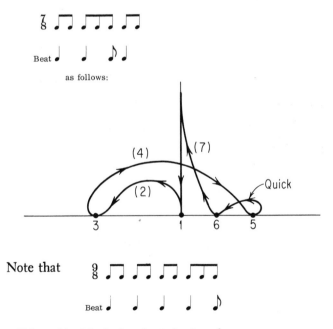

as follows:

Note that

would be a ⅝ with the last beat shortened.

Many people have trouble with these rhythms when they meet them for the first time. They sound jazzy, but are totally different (in traditional jazz the unit always remains the same and the syncopations vary around it). Take them slowly, conduct "slow motion" as described on page 57, and COUNT THE SHORTEST NOTES PRESENT. That is, in the examples above, on no account think a mixture of quarter and eighth notes, even though that is what your hand is beating. THINK EIGHTHS CONSTANTLY.

On innumerable occasions the writer has watched students doing this type of rhythm well and then noticed that the beat got slightly "off" and was hard to play to; in post mortems the student almost always admitted having stopped counting eighth notes at the very spot that his beat became inexact.

ASSIGNMENTS

Beginners:

1. Try the above and similar examples slowly, tapping as described on page 32, and counting eighth notes.
2. Conduct *Lark* by Aaron Copland (SATB: E.C. Schirmer). It provides an inexpensive introduction to this problem.
   (*Note:* In *Lark*, top of p. 12, the downbeats are so varied that the conductor gives the most help by not conducting at all. On p. 13, fill in the dotted lines and add time signatures before applying the techniques described in this chapter.)

Professionals:

1. Conduct:

2. When you are secure in the problems described in this chapter, try Britten's *Rejoice in the Lamb* (SATB and organ, Boosey and Hawkes). This is very difficult.

(*Note:* In the opening section the 6/8 bars are best done in 2; the 9/8 is usually a shortened 5/4, and the 11/8 a shortened 3/2.)

Note: The writer had a moderate tempo in mind for such examples as are given in this chapter—something in the general range of 130 to the quarter note. If the tempo is considerably faster, the alternative method should be used: beat quarters and dotted quarters, as the eighth note would be impossible to indicate. It may also be preferable to use this method even at moderate tempos when the rhythm is repeated at some length.

The first example on page 115 would be conducted as a 2 pattern, with the 2nd beat elongated in time; the next example would be a 3, with the 3rd beat elongated; the top of 117 would be a 3, with the 1st beat stretched, etc.

Sorry; I hope nobody dislocated a shoulder.

Chapter XXIV

THE AVANT-GARDE

The wave of new music called, for lack of a better name, the *avant-garde*, is sweeping away many barriers to the imagination of composers and performers. Rhythms, pitch combinations, and tone colors not previously heard in the concert hall are now part of our music. New philosophies are inspiring musicians. Musical notation is in a state of chaos as composers endeavor to find means of communicating their ideas to the performers.

When first confronted with an *avant-garde* score, a conductor is apt to think there is no link with the past. With increasing familiarity he will find that most of the devices in the new music have their roots in tradition. Although he will have much to learn that is new, standard conducting techniques will still play an important part, modified as required for each composition.

Three works for chorus and orchestra illustrate some new and old problems for the conductor. Stockhausen's *Momente* calls for an extraordinary variety of sounds and rhythms, written in symbols indecipherable without personal instruction. However, it is conducted using standard beat patterns, with a downbeat at the beginning of each heavy vertical line on the page. The difference from traditional music is that the beats are highly irregular in time and their spacing is shown proportionally in the score, with the timing given in seconds.

The Fragments of Archilochos, by Lukas Foss, is partly in standard notation and partly in the composer's own. It consists of twelve connected sections and is performed three times without pause. Although material is written for all the performers throughout the composition, the conductor selects beforehand only a comparatively small number of the performing forces to play during any one section. Thus there are hundreds of different possible versions of the piece. The musicians mark their own music, but have no way of knowing what else is to be played or sung at any one performance. At rehearsals for the premiere it proved extremely difficult for the "tacet" singers and instrumentalists to know when a new section started. The composer-conductor solved the problem by giving a large downbeat with his left hand at the start of each new section, as though slicing a huge cake.

Mauricio Kagel's *Diaphonie* is written entirely on slides. Two projectors are used, aimed at opposite sides of the stage, one for the orchestra, the other for the chorus. (At the premiere in Buffalo, Kagel operated the former and the writer the latter under the supervision of the composer.) The notation is original. When a slide is shown the respective performers begin to play or sing at their own time. They stop when the screen goes blank or if their part is obliterated. The density of performance is altered at will, either by holding pieces of cardboard in the projector's beam to cut off various sections of the group, or the conductor's fingers are dangled in front of the lens to reduce the density in a diffused manner. For one slide a tempo has to be set. This is done by beating time in front of the lens so as to cast a shadow on the screen at rhythmical intervals. It took considerable practice to move the arm at the proper rate of speed or the shadow was not seen; thus, the basic principle of beating time was followed, with a heavy shadow at the first beat of each bar!

At the same festival John Cage conducted his *Concert for Piano and Orchestra.* Instead of normal gestures, he moved his arms like the hands of a clock, to show how much time had elapsed. With *avant-garde* music it is frequently important to be able to sense elapsed time in seconds, where in traditional music it is necessary to think beats per minute.

Other works call for multiple conductors. Stockhausen's *Gruppen für drei Orchester* is for three conductors and three orchestras; his *Carrée* requires four choirs and orchestras, each with its own conductor, arranged at the four sides of a square auditorium, with the audience in the middle.

When a conductor starts to prepare an *avant-garde* work he must be sure to try traditional techniques thoroughly before abandoning or modifying them. Then, if necessary, he must experiment imaginatively and boldly in order to achieve in the new music the standard of performance expected in the old.

ASSIGNMENT

Beginners and Professionals:

1. If you have had little experience with *avant-garde* music, avail yourself of the first opportunity to hear or perform some representative examples. At first you may be shocked or amused, as most people have been with all innovations in music, from organum to Webern. In due course you will be able to assess and enjoy or reject various works as you would those in traditional style.

CHAPTER XXV

THE CONCERT

WARM-UP

Every instrumentalist looks upon it as his personal responsibility to warm up his instrument, fingers, reed, and embouchure. Amateur choristers, however, rarely have an opportunity to sing before a concert unless the conductor or choir master directs a general warm-up. This should consist of simple *vocalises* and straightforward singing, combined with suggestions for improving the tone. However, brains should not be neglected! Some fast or difficult passages should also be sung, and polished to a high degree. This speeds up the chorister's thinking and general mental tone, and will carry over into many other technical and artistic problems not covered in the warm-up, as described on page 108.

In addition to individual warm-up, if possible the orchestra or band should also have a short rehearsal an hour or so before the concert, especially when playing in a strange hall or if they did not rehearse earlier the same day. As with the chorus, this works wonders in improving alertness, reaction times, and general artistry.

Pre-concert warm-ups also afford a chance to steady a nervous group or arouse one that is tired or lethargic.

CONDUCTING FROM MEMORY

The conductor must be thoroughly familiar with every aspect of the music if he is to give a fine performance, but whether he dispenses with the score and music stand is another matter.

The ability to conduct from memory must be developed slowly. Do not attempt complex works until you have proved that you can memorize simple ones. Carols are easier than Beethoven symphonies, which in turn are easier than Handel oratorios or modern works. Recitatives are particularly bothersome.

When you study a score with a view to memorizing it be sure to analyze every detail, with special emphasis on sections which are alike for a while and then take different turns. Recapitulations are filled with death-traps.

When practising conducting from memory at home, provide visual distractions for yourself. Too often a musician memorizes in solitude and then may be thrown completely when something unusual happens at the concert, such as a trumpeter dropping his mute in the time-honored manner. See if you can conduct from memory while watching a football game on television with the sound turned off. While hard on the nerves and hardly conducive to the highest artistry, this will make the concert comparatively easy.

Do not conduct from memory in public unless you have done reasonably well without a score in rehearsals. Actually, they are harder than concerts, because the conductor constantly has in his mind such problems as how much time is left, whether to stop or keep going, how to improve the playing, etc. At a concert he is only concerned with the performance—or should be. Don't allow yourself to think about anything other than the music at hand. If you start planning how to acknowledge the soloists you may be in for a terrible jolt. CONCENTRATE!

If one has a secure knowledge of the music and the confidence to leave the score in the dressing room, there are great advantages in conducting from memory. The whole work is pictured at once, as well as any single page. While attending to details, it is still possible to see the relation of the details to the whole and to pace the performance accordingly. In Bach's Mass in B minor, for example, the individual movements seem grouped together into the main section of which they are a part; the Cum Sancto Spiritu is more closely related to the opening of the Gloria which it concludes than when merely seen in the score. This is a curious matter, and elusive to describe, but very real when one has experienced it.

Modern works are dangerous, but by the time a conductor has struggled with a score by Copland, Stravinsky, or Britten long enough to have memorized it securely, he is reasonably certain to have mastered the baton problems. Many passages in such works are so fast that they almost have to be memorized for the hand actions to come automatically.

Another advantage in conducting from memory is that a certain rapport grows between conductor and performers which rarely exists when there is a score between them. An almost hypnotic effect accumulates which can be overwhelming in a long work such as the Brahms Requiem, Handel's *Israel in Egypt*, Bach's Mass in B minor or Walton's *Belshazzar's Feast*. These intense moments provide the supreme artistic thrills for a conductor.

RE-CREATING THE MUSIC

Every time a conductor starts a concert he must realize that he is about to re-create a masterpiece of sound. No matter how much painstaking rehearsal has taken place he must infuse in the performers a desire to make every moment great. To be sure, there must be passages of relaxation and relief, but these should be great in their moderation. The conductor must do his utmost to bring out the best artistry in himself and the performers, but must also be clearly aware of all technical aspects. As has often been said, his heart must be on fire, but his brain must be on ice.

Don't get so excited that your fast tempos are unplayable; don't become so expressive that the wind players run out of air; bring out the cantabile theme in the cellos but don't wallow so that the horns can't play the syncopated accompaniment; don't grimace so that the singers' jaws tighten; whip the strings into a frenzy, but keep the downbeat clear so that the cymbal player can count his rests.

CONCERT CONDUCTING

No matter how many rehearsals are held, the concert is bound to be different. The conductor must be on continuous alert for the unexpected, and react immediately. (Even on tour, where the same program is given night after night, the variations from one concert to the next are multitudinous.) Excitement may improve one piece and lassitude spoil another. Balances are frequently altered. Listen constantly and adjust as required. The hall sounds different with an audience. The horns may have reverberated unduly in an empty hall and you suppressed them; with a full house they may be too muffled. You must hear the difference and bring them up a little. Some passages may be performed with greater or less confidence than before. You may have had trouble earlier making the strings play an adequate crescendo-diminuendo, and were forced to make your beat rather large; at the concert the players may be exceptionally responsive and overdo the effect. Tone down your gestures at such points.

Other unexpected problems may develop, some artistic, some technical, whatever the level of proficiency. The flute may miss an entrance; bring him in clearly at his next cue. The bassoon may come in early. Wave him off and help him enter at the proper place. The chorus may seem a little stale in an allegro; see if you can recapture some of the excitement of a few days earlier by moving the tempo a shade faster and at the same time exhorting them to greater heights with your arms, face, and will power.

The violas may run ahead on a figure that they had always played in strict time; turn away from what you usually conduct and give heavy, ponderous motions to slow them before chaos results. The contrabasses may lag; give them a scowl and some small, crisp beats. The choir's pitch may sag or sharp a little; try to raise or lower it with your left hand.

You may suddenly realize that a certain movement in rehearsal has been monotonously close in tempo to its immediate predecessor; the scales fall from your eyes (and ears) and you take it more slowly and expressively, thrilled with a new beauty you had not anticipated.

The soprano soloist, a pillar of icy poise all week, may be trembling with fear; give her a smile and some confident cues. The tenors may sing a melody too jerkily; make smooth, flowing motions in their direction with your left arm while your right continues to give angular accents to the cellos. The first trombone may blow a blooper; a grin will probably set him at ease and he'll be all right for the rest of the concert. Since the last rehearsal the snare drummer has practised a tricky part, previously barely audible, and is now playing it with ear-splitting gusto; catch his eye and give him the "sh" sign before the ceiling comes down.

These illustrations show the variety of thoughts that race through a conductor's mind during a performance. It would be interesting to know the speed of thought under such conditions, compared with other professions. It is this ability to listen, think fast, and communicate with hands, arms, and face that marks the good concert conductor, as contrasted to the good musician who can train performers. He combines artistry, knowledge, and sensitivity with speed of thought and action to re-create the music every time he conducts.

The ability to think fast is probably innate, but doubtless can be improved through practice. Obviously, if conducting technique as described in this book has been developed to a high degree so that it is almost instinctive, and if the conductor's musical ability and knowledge of the score are also at a high level, a greater percentage of his attention can be spent on re-creating the music and handling emergencies. However, the only real way to learn how to conduct a concert, as opposed to a rehearsal, is—conduct concerts!

ASSIGNMENTS

Beginners and Professionals:

1. From time to time in the months ahead review this book and see if you can catch yourself deviating from any of its recommended practices. If so, reconsider them. Perhaps your instincts are right and the book is wrong. Perhaps certain circumstances warrant departing from rule. Or, on the other hand, *perhaps you've developed a fault!*
2. CONDUCT!

INDEX